The Art and Science of Vedic Astrology

THE ART AND SCIENCE OF VEDIC ASTROLOGY

RICHARD FISH & RYAN KURCZAK

ISBN-13: 978-1475267655

Asheville Vedic Astrology
Asheville, NC
Telephone 828-423-6636
Email: ryan@ashevillevedicastrology.com
web site: www.ashevillevedicastrology.com

CONTENTS

Introduction

The purpose of this book is to present a basic course in astrological technique and astrological knowledge, while providing a functional framework for the development of the intuitive capabilities characteristic of a competent astrologer. Astrological rules, the meanings of planets, houses, signs and their interrelationships form the body, the structure of astrology. The creative intelligence organizes the information and reveals the message of the horoscope to the astrologer. The full value of astrology is realized when the two unite.

In this regard, to be an astrologer requires sufficient intellectual skill to comprehend the concepts presented. In the words of Sri Yukteswar, "Astrology is too vast, both mathematically and philosophically, to be rightly grasped except by men of profound understanding. If ignoramuses misread the heavens and see there a scrawl instead of a script that is to be expected in this imperfect world. One should not dismiss the wisdom with the wise."

With the advent of computer programs, much of the mathematical calculations no longer present a barrier. However, one intent on astrological study may still need to strengthen the mental faculty. If the mind does not initially comprehend the material, it will with time, intention to understand, and repeated exposure.

To the uninitiated, a Vedic astrological chart looks like a square, sectioned into twelve portions and randomly peppered with glyphs. Each section has a particular meaning. Each glyph represents a sign or a planet. Depending on what sections of the chart the glyphs fall and where they are relative to each other, many meanings are possible.

What takes one from an arm chair philosopher and makes them into an astrologer with valid insight?

A teacher is helpful. Anytime one converses with a person of skill and merit in a chosen field, learning is possible. By remembering the instruction of the teacher, knowledge is imparted directly. There is also a natural tendency to become like the company one keeps. Not only can teachers share knowledge and experience, they can also share their presence. When no teachers are available, the right study of books can serve the purpose.

Volumes have been written on astrology. The more one reads and commits to memory the multitudinous meanings of astrological variables, the deeper the reservoir of knowledge that is available for evaluating the horoscope. Add to that curiosity to discern the essence, or energetic signature, each variable represents and then the intuition begins to grow.

Vedic Astrology is best practiced by a person whose awareness is clear and whose intuition is highly developed. To this end, yogic meditation and lifestyle, which facilitate clarity of awareness, is recommended. More will be said about relevant yogic methods and philosophy later in the book.

Mastery provides a means for greater self-awareness. The more one learns about the planetary movements through the heavens and the relationship between sky and earth the more inclined one is to perceive that consciousness is a seamless whole.

The ultimate goal of Vedic astrology is to reveal the manifest nature of reality, as it is, beyond hopes, dreams, or delusions. People have different experiences in life. When they can make peace with where they are and make the best of the situations that are available to them, they can be freed from suffering. No longer prodded by obsessions or compulsions, they can act appropriately, naturally, and spontaneously.

Astrology and Self-Realization

The purpose of Vedic Astrology is to promote Self-realization. It encourages awareness of one's essence of being as superior to the transient phenomena with which most people identify, such as circumstances, personality and the body.

It teaches, "Here are the trends of your life, the life experiences you sustain through behaving in the same ways repeatedly. If you keep living in the same way, here is an estimate of how your life will unfold. Now that you know the patterns you can change them, because the patterns are not you." When one is tired of feigning helplessness and confusion in life, Vedic Astrology outlines a way to responsibility and success. Verse sixteen of chapter two in the Yoga Sutras of Patanjali reads, "Pain which has not yet manifested is to be avoided." When you can avoid the pain, you free up your energy to focus on being a productive, conscious human being. Then your absolute and relative purposes are integrated.

Vedic Astrology is a spiritual discipline and the practice of enlightened living improves an astrologer's ability to adhere to that discipline. It requires neutrality, objectivity, the ability to see and speak the truth, and the compassion to share information without inciting fear or emotional distress. Through meditation and practice of the yamas and niyamas outlined in Yogic literature, these qualities become manifest in the astrologer. Then the act of practicing astrology assists in clarifying the awareness of others.

It is important to note that superstitious reliance on astrological information dilutes the potency of the information provided. Looking to the position of the planets for answers to every decision made in life serves no purpose. Self-realized souls are guided by an inner knowing. Prior to Self-realization, we should do everything we can to encourage that inner knowing. If every challenge impels us to consult the planetary transits or the astrological chart, we are not allowing our own inner knowing to develop. When a person is sincerely in need of guidance, an astrologer can provide that guidance.

Astrology As Vedic Knowledge

All knowledge is within consciousness. As individualized units of Infinite Consciousness, the potential for all knowledge is within every human being. The sages and seers of old knew this truth. By studying the movements of the planets through space and the patterns they made, the sages realized that the state of the solar system reflected the nature of the circumstances in the moment. By understanding the cosmic influences, they could then relate appropriately to what life presented. Seeing the cosmos reflected within their own being, it became apparent that their own being was reflected within the cosmos. To know the reason why things happened as they did, they could look within or to the sky. Both led to the realization of the Self, and to a higher knowledge called the Veda.

When we know the fullness of our real Self, beyond delusions and illusions, we become a knower of the Veda. We are then Self-realized, enlightened. Established in our Self, our actions flow spontaneously. We know we are not the doer, but the contact point with creation through which consciousness expresses itself. Our actions are appropriate because impelled by the knowledge of our Self, the Self that is aware of all things and is in harmony with life. The Infinite Consciousness, or the Self, is naturally inclined towards harmony.

Yoga and Ayurveda

Vedic Astrology shares its roots with Yoga and Ayurveda. All three are sister sciences with one ultimate aim: to provide the proper structure in the physical world to allow the clarity of Self-realization to flow freely into material creation. Yoga provides physical and mental practices to tame the mind and the restlessness of the body. Ayurvedic lifestyle regimens harmonize the individualized mind/body constitution for optimal physical functioning. Vedic Astrology reveals the map and timing of habits and tendencies that may manifest in our life experiences. All for the purpose of elevating our awareness above the pull of the unconscious influences that can keep us bound to sorrow, grief and repeated needless suffering.

Considered the eye of the Vedas, Vedic Astrology plays a unifying role in the enlightened sciences given to us by the ancients. Through Vedic Astrology we can see our Ayurvedic constitution, the timing and potential for disease and health, and the times to take extra care of our bodies. Yoga is more than just the holding of physical postures or sitting in meditation. It is a way of life for the purpose of complete and total spiritual liberation from the dream of mortality. In this regard, everything we do either supports or negates that liberation. Vedic Astrology can reveal the self-defeating tendencies we may not be aware of so we can gain control of our situation. It shows us the strengths we have to build on for success in both mundane and spiritual worlds. Since there is no division between the mundane and spiritual, success in one realm synergistically supports success in the other. Until we are fully awake in the knowledge of the Self, Vedic Astrology is an invaluable tool to this end.

Clarifying Awareness

The study of Vedic Astrology clarifies awareness. This helps to bring us closer to our eternal nature, which is infinite pure consciousness, by revealing our interconnectedness with the whole of reality. The planets move through the zodiac and the currents generated reflect in our daily lives and mind sets. We may look for the reasons, the whys, the causes of our circumstances and find the nearest person or situation to blame.

The more effective our study of astrology, the clearer is our understanding that our immediate surroundings are not the reasons for how we feel or what we are experiencing. We discover the opposite, that our feelings and inner states of being create the external experience. The movement of the planets can only trigger what is already within us. The study of the birth chart shows the nature and location of the triggers that create our reality. This is why one person may be in the exact same situation and see it differently. The inner state of person "A" is different than person "B", and this is apparent in the horoscope.

The clearer our awareness, the more easily we can relate to life, because we then see life as it is, rather than what we think it is. To know the triggers that are within us allows us to remove our identification from them. No longer identified with the internal causes of unconscious or compulsive actions, we can choose to act appropriately in the situation.

People often look to their quirks or idiosyncrasies as treasured extensions of their self whether they are useful or not. Vedic Astrology points beyond the personality. It shows that our personality is a temporary manifestation of the habits we maintain. While embodied, the personality is a reference point for consciousness to interact within the time-space continuum. By knowing this, a person can let go of useless tendencies that serve no purpose other than to stubbornly settle into a rut of constant painful experiences. From here, the freedom to live spontaneously arises. The will is emboldened and the power to choose worthwhile circumstances is strengthened. In this way, the astrologer helps to guide the evolution of consciousness towards complete spiritual liberation.

"Karmic influences exist because of a mistaken sense of Self and the support of objects of perception. In their absence, karmic influences disappear."
–Yoga Sutras of Patanjali 4:11

Fate Versus Freewill

The astrological birth chart can indicate the tendencies and habits we have sustained from previous births. As children, we typically react to life based on these patterns. As we grow older, wiser and more conscious, we realize our experiences in life are based on perceptions and our reactions to what occurs.

When we become conscious of our situation, of where we are in life, we can then make changes for the better. The more unconscious a person is, the less likely their experiences will change through time. The greater the degree of consciousness, the more inclined they will be to make appropriate changes when needed. In this regard, one is fated to experience karmic situations until responsibility is accepted, in the present, for actions and states of consciousness.

When responsibility has been accepted, we can alter the influences within the birth chart and experience the higher manifestation of the planetary energies. Once the higher manifestations have been actualized, we can move beyond even that and attune with the source of the planetary energies and the source of all creation.

Responsibility can be accepted and the karmic habits erased and nullified by various means. The two most important remedial measures include Yogic meditation and behavior modification. Vedic astrology also provides planetary remedies using faultless gemstones, planetary mantras, color therapy, aromatherapy, and combinations of precious metals.

Through yoga meditation we can learn to no longer identify with our habits, feelings, memories, bodies, relationships or thoughts. Since most people are identified with these conditions, they are seldom inclined to make life changes because altering these aspects that they identify with would threaten their false sense of self. By meditation, attention is turned away from these outward manifestations and internalized to directly experience the pure eternal essence of being that is beyond identification with transient experiences.

In time, experiencing the joy of being through meditation provides the perspective that is needed to let go of attachment with which we formerly identified. Altering our path in life then becomes easier, because we are no longer invested in maintaining the false sense of self and are more inclined to act in harmony with the whole of creation.

Behavior modification is one of the most practical means of pacifying karmic planetary energy. In the Yoga Sutras of Patanjali, the first two limbs of yoga practice, before the practice of meditation, asana practice, and breathing exercises are the yamas and niyamas. These are the main external and internal means of behavior modification that provide the first steps to freedom from planetary influence.

"Refraining from harmful behaviors, faithful adherence to constructive practices, firm meditation posture, pranayama practice, internalized attention, concentration, meditation, and samadhi are the eight limbs of yoga practice."
 -*Yoga Sutras of Patanjali* 2:29

The yamas include nonviolence, truth, nonstealing, conservation of vital forces, and nonpossessiveness. The yamas are the external practices, which are to be incorporated during daily living. The niyamas include purity, contentment, intensity in spiritual practice, practice of learned personal mantras, and alignment of attention with the Eternal Self—the witnessing consciousness. The niyamas are the internal practices, used to change our states of consciousness.

Prescription of gemstones, mantras, color therapy, aromatherapy and wearing of precious metals are a secondary support to ameliorating planetary influences. More will be said on these practices in the chapter on remedial measures.

CHAPTER ONE

STUDY AND PRACTICE

The Role of the Astrologer

The astrologer's role is threefold: to serve as an objective witness, bringing to light the hidden aspects of a client's life; a guide, showing the way to success based on astrological influences; and to provide a map for harmonizing the four main purposes of human life.

Astrology provides a glimpse into the areas of life that are fully supported and that a client might be taking for granted. It can also show areas that are weak and need strengthening through remedial measures.

Vedic astrology may indicate when to perform actions that are supportive of particular endeavors. Imagine a client expressing interest in moving to another country and starting a new business. Success for that endeavor could be indicated in the chart, but the astrological influences do not indicate success for the venture until five years. If an astrologer did not share this information with the client, the client might make the move and start the business only to struggle needlessly for several years.

Human beings incarnate to fulfill four main purposes in life:

· Proper livelihood in accordance with our abilities.
· The ability to have resources for our needs.
· Enjoyment of our life circumstances.
· Liberation of consciousness from the mistaken sense of individual isolated existence.

To fulfill these purposes we need knowledge to recognize what our available resources are or how to acquire them; how to understand our capacities to achieve goals; and how the trends of life will unfold to make the best of supportive times and prepare for the leaner times. Until we are aware and able to turn within to access this knowledge directly, Vedic astrology may reveal what is hidden and provide the information needed.

Promoting the Four Goals of Life

Many people wonder about their real purpose in life. When we know that we are meant to be spiritually enlightened, we can implement actions, such as meditation practice, to make it easier. Our relative purpose, the work we are here to do, is reflected in the birth chart, and may be a variation of the activities in which we are already engaged.

The ideal is to harness the higher influences of the cosmic forces, and eliminate the baser effects. A person with a strong Mars and other contributing influences in the birth chart could become a violent individual who likes to burn things down. That would be the baser influence of the cosmic forces. The higher influence of such patterns could be reflected in a person who is a soldier defending the helpless or a fighter of forest fires. Either way the influences of fire and violence indicated by Mars are in effect. They are being directed in qualitatively different ways.

Regarding financial security, many of us have different sub-conscious influences that direct us to either easily acquire wealth or to unconsciously resist it. The causes of the shortages may be found in the horoscope. A Vedic astrologer can see what in the chart is preventing the acquisition of needed resources. This can be due to the particular time in a person's life, a faulty belief system, or to the lack of constructive endeavor or receptivity.

Proper Study

The first step to becoming a Vedic astrologer is learning the material by reading, memorization, and repeated exposure. Have a journal for taking notes on what you read. Rewriting what you learn will help impress the information in your mind.

Do not rush through the process. Make flash cards to look at. When you are comfortable with an understanding of the planets, houses, and signs, look at your birth chart or the chart of someone you know well. See where the planets are placed. Keep your observations general. Think about the various areas of your life such as career, home life, or personal relationships. Look at the specific houses in the chart that represent those areas in your life. For example, do you see Mars placed in your seventh house, the house of personal relationships? Does that reflect any intensiveness in your relationship with other people? Do you see Jupiter in your 4th house? Does that reflect happy feelings you have for home? Or is Rahu in the 4th house influencing you to dislike being home and causing a sense of insatiable wanderlust in your psyche?

You can then refine your observations with subtler details. For example, maybe you do have Mars in your seventh house. Is Mars in the same house as Venus? This could suggest a romantic attraction in a relationship. Is Mars with Saturn? This is totally different, and could bring out a cruel and angry side to your relationships. Both show the fire of Mars in relationship, but Mars becomes influenced by the loving side of Venus or the harsh side of Saturn.

Compare your actual life experiences and see how they are reflected in the chart. Once you can easily match up your life with the chart, you can start looking at the charts of people you do not know and make accurate observations.

Practice

As you acquire experience you will begin to trust what you see in the chart. When you trust what you see, you are strengthening your intuition. The more you trust what is seen, the more often you will be correct in your observations. Through the astrological chart you will be privy to deeper information about the client. The average person is a psychological mixture of contradictions and idiosyncrasies. You, and the client, will be surprised at what you can discern with a casual glance.

Mistakes will be made. Treat them as learning experiences. You may be incorrect when you first attempt a reading, or perhaps the client will not want to admit that you are right. Trust your intuition and speak it if it seems appropriate to the session. If it does not seem appropriate, make a note about what you have seen. It may become appropriate during another reading.

Do not say more than you are inspired to say. Beginning astrologers are often nervous about giving a reading, and talk more than is necessary. The client needs to have helpful information.

An experienced astrologer can sense truth. When an insight from the chart flashes into the astrologer's mind he can think about saying that to the client and feel an inner response. Inner responses will either be positive, indicating the information is valid, or flat, indicating it is not important or not true.

An astrological reading may confirm what the client already knows about troublesome situations. An astrologer then needs to be familiar with the alignment of the planets that may contribute to the problems. The astrologer needs to see how a retrograde malefic Saturn or the lord of the second and seventh house could be creating strife and pain. The astrologer also needs to know how to learn to work with those influences to relieve the burden. This may involve mantra practice or an astrological gem. Or it may require the client to change the way they think or behave. The astrologer's job requires care and compassion in sharing what is seen as clearly as possible.

CHAPTER TWO

MEDITATION AND ASTROLOGY

Meditation is helpful to being a good astrologer. Meditation clears the mind of conditionings and elevates awareness above the influence of samskaras (mental impressions with the potential to influence experiences). Samskaras are like impurities in glass. The more impurities, the harder it is to see the world on the other side correctly, or in this case, the nature of the horoscope in question. Someone trying to practice astrology with substantial mental conditioning is more inclined to see his own story reflected in the chart, rather than the truth about the person seeking guidance. An astrologer needs to be able to look at the client's chart, assess the client's current condition, and provide useful information as clearly as possible.

The Vedic astrologer knows that he is only influenced by karma to the degree that he identifies with it. Having this realization, he can then teach his clients the techniques that worked for him and encourage them to rise above their karma as well. The astrologer's purpose is not fortune telling or entertainment; it is to show the client how to live effectively.

Daily meditation practice is recommended for the astrologer, as well as meditation before examining a chart and before giving an astrological reading. A client should also be encouraged to meditate before the session.

When practiced with attention, the following meditation techniques are effective in eliciting superconsciousness and can be used by anyone. Beginning meditators are advised to sit for twenty minutes once or twice a day. Proficient meditators can sit for forty five minutes or longer, as long as the practice is alert and attentive. Passive daydreaming, slipping into subconscious states, or sleeping are not useful.

Set aside the same time each day for meditation practice so that it becomes part of your regular routine.

Dedicating a place in the house or a special chair for meditation practice is also useful. It may help to have a ritual, such as lighting a candle or saying a prayer. Consistently practice the techniques until you can be superconscious.

Basic Mantra Meditation

Sitting up straight and comfortable, bring your awareness to your breathing. Take a deep breath and exhale, letting your body relax while keeping your head and neck erect. Then let the breath flow in and out naturally. Do not force the breathing. Simply observe it.

Once settled and focused on the breath, introduce the mantra "so hum." Mentally chant the mantra. Hear the sound "so" resonating within your field of awareness on the inhale. Mentally listen to the sound "hum" resonating within your field of awareness on the exhale. To fully engage your attention in this process, imagine each syllable vibrating within your being.

Let your awareness be drawn further inward on each inhalation and exhalation. In time, thoughts and emotions will settle and you will experience inner peace. When this occurs, ignore the mantra. Sit in the peace generated by practice. If thoughts, memories, or emotions emerge, repeat the technique to reestablish your inner poise.

"One should vocally and mentally chant Om, attentively listen to it, meditatively contemplate it, comprehend its real nature, and identify with it."
– *Yoga Sutras of Patanjali 1:28*

Inner Light and Sound Contemplation

In Vedic teachings Om is considered the primordial vibration that emanates from the source of creation. Meditate on Om to restore your awareness to its original pure wholeness. Om can be chanted audibly or mentally. It can also be contemplated by gazing into the spiritual eye and listening to subtle sound frequencies around the head.

In a quiet place with little external light, assume a meditation posture. Take a few deep breaths, relaxing your body on each exhale.

Once settled, bring your attention up to the higher brain centers. Be aware of the space between your eyebrows and the crown of the head. With your eyes closed, gaze into the darkness of your closed eyelids. Imagine the darkness has depth and space. Lift your gaze slightly upward as if looking at the top of a distant mountain. Continue to gaze off through the dark inner space of your closed eyes.

Now, listen for an inner sound current within your ear. It may sound like a high pitched hum, a ringing, or another constant tone. Examine this sound. Listen for any change in the sound. Listen behind the sound. Do you hear another sound behind it? Does the one you are listening to get louder? Continue to follow the sounds as they change and draw you deeper into meditation.

With practice, the electrical activity of the nervous system you are listening to, will enable you to hear the Om vibration. Allow your small sense of self to dissolve into the sounds you perceive.

As you practice this technique, while keeping your attention in the higher brain centers and looking inward, you may also begin to see lights or geometrical patterns in your spiritual eye. When this occurs, let them attract your attention. Contemplating inner light may enable you to more easily hear the Om vibration. As you go deeper into the sound current, look through the inner light. Feel that you are piercing the light, as if you are moving through your forehead into the source of the light.

Just as the initial sounds you hear around your head are the electrical activity of the nervous system, initial light perceptions are the result of brain activity. To practice inner light and sound contemplation you may want to practice the basic mantra technique first. The calmer and more internalized you are, the easier it will be.

"Japa (mantra repitition) is affirmation and concentrated verbal communion with the divine energies that work to change one's consciousness and one's life."
– *Ernst Wilhelm, the Graha Sutras*

Astrology Specific Meditation Techniques

Our karma is reflected in the planetary alignments. There are outward actions, such as providing specific services to the people of the world and giving of charity to particular individuals, that help to alleviate karma, but it is much better to work on the karma directly through meditation. Harmonizing and pacifying our inner cosmos eases our passage through the outer cosmos by reciprocity.

The *chakras* along the spinal pathway have correlations to the planets and signs. From the top of the head to the base of the spine runs a subtle astral channel called *sushumna*, the radiant path. By giving attention to this pathway and the *chakras* the higher influences of the planets may be encouraged to manifest in our lives and the seeds of negative karma neutralized.

The following charts illustrate the correlation between the chakras, planets and signs:

Correlation of the Planets to the Chakras

Chakra	Planet
Spiritual Eye	Sun/Moon
Throat Chakra	Mercury
Heart Chakra	Venus
Navel Chakra	Mars
Sacrum Chakra	Jupiter
Root Chakra	Saturn

Correlation of the Zodiac Signs to the Chakras

Chakra	Zodiacal Sign
Spiritual Eye	Cancer/Leo
Throat Chakra	Gemini/Virgo
Heart Chakra	Taurus/Libra
Navel Chakra	Aries/Scorpio
Sacrum Chakra	Pisces/Sagittarius
Root Chakra	Aquarius/Capricorn

Any form of meditation that elicits superconsciousness has a cleansing effect on our karma, but two meditation techniques directly influence the *sushumna*. It is best to practice the following techniques after using the basic mantra technique to internalize your awareness.

Chanting Through the Chakras

Sit upright in a meditation posture. Bring your attention to the base of your spine. Maintain your attention there for 5 to 10 breaths. Bring your attention up to the second chakra. Rest there for a few moments. Continue bringing your attention up through the *chakras* to the crown *chakra*. As you go up through the *chakras*, mentally chant the appropriate mantra at each *chakra*.

Chakra	Location	Mantric Syllable
Root	Base of the spine	Lum
Sacrum	Small of the back	Vum
Navel	Behind the navel	Rum
Heart	Between the shoulder blades	Yum
Throat	Back of the neck	Hum
Third Eye	Between the eyebrows	Om
Crown	Higher brain	Om

Then go down to the base of your spine chanting the mantra at each chakra. Repeat the procedure two or three times. Conclude your practice at the crown *chakra*.

***Sushumna* Breathing**

The birth chart is considered to be static. As planets move, they trigger various *karmic* influences indicated by the birth chart. Circulating life force through the spine quickens the process of evolution.

To practice *sushumna* breathing, meditate as you normally do. When the mind is calm and emotions settled, put your attention in your spine. Feel your spine, from the base to the crown chakra. Imagine a hollow tube within the spine.

Breathe slightly deeper than normal and in a relaxed manner. As you inhale, use a gentle act of will to pull your life force up through the hollow tube in your spine. If you do not feel a sensation of prana ascending through the spine, imagine what it would feel like. When the inhalation is complete the pranic current will be in the crown *chakra*. Hold your breath for a second, and then exhale easily and without force while noting the descending flow of the current. Let the breath exhale of its own accord. Do not force the breath out. Let the energetic current flow back down your spine like water.

When silence prevails in your awareness and you are absorbed in existence-being, pull the current up to the top of the head one last time. Let your breathing occur naturally. Keep the current and your attention in the crown *chakra*. Sit in the silence until you conclude your meditation practice.

Basic Mantra Meditation – Astrological Variations

The basic mantra meditation technique can be modified to focus on specific planetary energies. By using the following mantras on the appropriate day, the astrologer attunes to and harmonizes with the seed essence of the planet. With consistent practice this will result in the astrologer gaining a deeper understanding of the planets. The study of descriptions of the planets in books is good, but direct contact with the planetary energies through mantric meditation is better.

The days ruled by the planets and their respective mantras are as follows:

Sunday	The Sun	"Om Soom"
Monday	The Moon	"Om Soam"
Tuesday	Mars	"Om Koom"
Wednesday	Mercury	"Om Boom"
Thursday	Jupiter	"Om Goom"
Friday	Venus	"Om Shoom"
Saturday	Saturn	"Om Shum"

The South Node of the Moon, Ketu, is related to Tuesday because of its likeness to Mars. Ketu's mantra is *Om Kame*. The North Node of the Moon, Rahu, is related to Saturday. Rahu's mantra is *Om Rum*.

To practice these planetary mantras, substitute the mantra for the day for *So Hum*.

"Aum Shri Ganeshaya Namaha"
-Salutions to Ganesha, The Lord of Astrology-
"Aum Vakrathunda Mahakaya Soorya Koti Samaprabha nirvignam Kuru Mey DevaSarva Karyeshu Sarvada"

-Salutations to the curved trunked, huge bodied lord, who is lit like a million Sun's, please remove our obstacles from all our undertakings-

CHAPTER THREE

FUNDAMENTAL TERMINOLOGY

"Though various well written works on astrology, the productions of able men, exist for the enlightenment of the student of astrology, I begin to construct this small boat consisting of stanzas written in various metres and of several meanings for those persons attempting to cross the vast ocean of astrology."
– Brihat Jataka 1:2

Beginners often find the study of *Jyotish* (Vedic Astrology) overwhelming while assimilating the needed information to understand and judge the indications of an astrological chart. We have attempted to present this information in a clear, straightforward, and logical manner. Once you have thoroughly assimilated the basic qualities of the planets, signs, and houses all the other details tend to fall naturally into place and are easier to understand.

Terminology

For the first half of the book, we will use the equivalent English words, along with the transliterated Sanskrit terms, italicized. Sometimes there is no one word in English that suitably conveys the meaning of the Sanskrit, in such a case, only the Sanskrit term will be used.

Key points regarding the differences between
Jyotish and Western Astrology

The most obvious difference between the two systems is that Western astrology uses the Tropical or "moving" zodiac, whereas Vedic astrology uses the Sidereal or "fixed" zodiac, which corresponds to the actual star constellations. This means that the position of the Ascendant and of each planet, as calculated for a Western birth chart, must move backward approximately 23 degrees to be converted into the Sidereal zodiac. This shift backwards is known as the *Ayanamsha*. It is quite likely that your Sun, Moon or Ascendant will fall back into the previous sign when your chart is converted from the Western to the Vedic system. The Vedic approach to sign interpretation is very different from the Western one, and will present no basic contradictions.

In *Jyotish* much emphasis is placed on the position of planets in houses, while the sign positions are studied to understand the strengths and weaknesses of the planets. In Western Astrology the signs are given more importance, especially in determining the character and personality of an individual. Thus the information extracted from a planet's sign position in *Jyotish* is rather different from the information that a Western astrologer extracts from its position in the Tropical zodiac.

In traditional Vedic astrology the whole of the Rising Sign (or Ascendant) constitutes the first house, the whole of the following sign constitutes the second house. If Libra is the Ascending sign, the whole 30 degrees of Libra constitutes the first house, the whole of Scorpio constitutes the second house, and so on. This is known as the "House equals Sign" method. Some Vedic astrologers employ the Indian "Sripati" system of house division, which also takes the Midheaven as the cusp of the 10th house. However, the vast majority use the "House equals Sign" method, just as the vast majority of Western astrologers use one of the Quadrant systems.

At first sight the "House equals Sign" system may appear to be a rather crude method of house division. The more familiar you become with the system, the more you will appreciate its relevance and applicability, especially when one considers the common practice in Vedic astrology of using a variety of "divisional charts." These are similar to the Harmonic charts developed by the astrologer John Addey, which were partially inspired by his studies of the divisional charts of Vedic astrology. Vedic astrologers can use up to 15 divisional charts, all of which are derived from the main *(rashi)* chart, each giving insight into a particular area of a person's life. For example the 10th divisional chart, the *Dashamsa*, provides additional information regarding a person's career, while the 12th division chart, the *Dwadamsa*, provides insight into one's parents, ancestral heritage and past life karma. The most used divisional chart is the *Navamsha,* which corresponds with the 9th Harmonic chart now used by some Western astrologers. The *Navamsha* is nearly as important as the *Rashi* or main sign chart, and gives additional information regarding long term relationships. It is also used to determine whether the indications of the natal chart are going to manifest with difficulty or ease. Esoteric astrologers regard the *Navamsha* as the horoscope of the soul, and the *Rashi* or main sign chart as representing the outer and more mundane conditions of a person's life.

Traditional Vedic astrology does not include the more recently discovered outer planets – Uranus, Neptune and Pluto, although some modern practitioners *do* take them into account. More importance is attached to the North and South Nodes of the Moon, (known as *Rahu* and *Ketu*). If including the outer planets (and experience shows that they can provide invaluable insights), the modern attribution of their sign rulerships should be ignored. Thus the ruler of Scorpio is always Mars rather than Pluto, Aquarius is ruled by Saturn rather than Uranus, and Pisces is ruled by Jupiter rather than Neptune. The modern rulerships may be valid in Western astrology but their use would create confusion and cloud judgement if used in Vedic astrology. The use of Planetary *Yogas* is unique in this system of astrology. A *yoga* in the context of astrology means a union or combination of certain planetary factors. There are many hundreds of *yogas* mentioned in the classical Sanskrit texts, and the study of these *yogas* can be most enlightening, often giving insight into important details of a person's character or circumstances that could not otherwise be explained.

Books on Jyotish

If you intend to purchase books as supplementary study material to this text it is recommended that you make a start with those by western authors on the subject. Later you can try tackling those written by modern Indian authors, and eventually you may want to acquire some of the classical source texts translated into English. Below are our personal recommendations. The six source books listed are perhaps the most important and influential classical astrological texts.

Western Authors:
Astrology of the Seers by David Frawley
Beneath a Vedic Sky by William Levacy
Ancient Hindu Astrology for Modern Western Astrologers by
      James Braha
Light on Life by Defouw & Svoboda

Indian Authors:
Books by Dr. K. S. Charak
Books by B.V. Raman

Recommended Primary Source Textbooks:
Brihat Parashara Hora Shastra by Parashara
Saravali by Kalyana Vara
Brihat Jataka by Viraha Mihira
Hora Sara by Prithuyashas
Phaldeepika by Mantreshwara
Sarvatha Chintamani by Venkatesha Daivanga

Calculating the Astrological Chart

Any astrology computer program will make these calculations for you, saving much time and effort. Those who are seriously committed to the study and practice Jyotish are likely to end up buying a quality Vedic computer program. If learning the process from a book, for simplicity purchase one on Western astrology, calculate the chart, and then convert it to a Vedic chart.

Ayanamsha

On the next page is a table that gives the number of degrees that need to be deducted from the position of the planets and Ascendant point calculated for the Tropical Zodiac in order arrive at their positions in the Sidereal Zodiac. This will be useful if you already have a chart calculated by a Western astrologer or if you possess a Western ephemeris (an ephemeris is a publication listing the daily positions of the planets).

There are small differences of opinion as to the exact starting point of the Sidereal zodiac, so *ayanamsha* tables can show small variations. In common with the majority of Vedic astrologers we are using the Lahiri *Ayanamsha* (also known as the *Chaitrapaksha Ayanamsha*) that we find to be the most reliable.

Let us suppose that you have to convert a western birth chart for someone born in 1976. Refer to the figures given for that year (see table), which is 23° (degrees) 31' (minutes). Simply deduct this number of degrees and minutes from all the zodiacal positions that are shown in the western chart or ephemeris.

LAHIRI'S AYANAMSHA 1900 to 2030

1900	22°	28'	1933	22°	56'	1966	23	23
1901	22	29	1934	22	56	1967	23	24
1902	22	29	1935	22	57	1968	23	25
1903	22	30	1936	22	58	1969	23	25
1904	22	31	1937	22	59	1970	23	26
1905	22	32	1938	23	0	1971	23	27
1906	22	33	1939	23	1	1972	23	28
1907	22	33	1940	23	1	1973	23	29
1908	22	34	1941	23	2	1974	23	30
1909	22	35	1942	23	3	1975	23	31
1910	22	36	1943	23	4	1976	23	31
1911	22	37	1944	23°	4'	1977	23°	32'
1912	22	38	1945	23	5	1978	23	33
1913	22	39	1946	23	6	1979	23	34

Year	°	'	Year	°	'	Year	°	'
1914	22	40	1947	23	7	1980	23	35
1915	22	40	1948	23	8	1981	23	36
1916	22	41	1949	23	9	1982	23	36
1917	22	42	1950	23	10	1983	23	37
1918	22	43	1951	23	11	1984	23	38
1919	22	44	1952	23	11	1985	23	39
1920	22	45	1953	23	12	1986	23	40
1921	22	46	1954	23	13	1987	23	41
1922	22	46	1955	23	14	1988	23°	41'
1923	22	47	1956	23	15	1989	23	42
1924	22	48	1957	23	16	1990	23	43
1925	22	49	1958	23	17	1991	23	44
1926	22	49	1959	23	17	1992	23	45
1926	22	50	1960	23	18	1993	23	46
1928	22	51	1961	23	19	1994	23	46
1929	22	52	1962	23	19	1995	23	47
1930	22	53	1963	23	20	1996	23	48
1931	22	54	1964	23	21	1997	23	49
1932	22	55	1965	23	22	1998	23	50
1999	23	51	2010	24	0	2021	24°	9'
2000	23	51	2011	24	0	2022	24	10
2001	23	52	2012	24	1	2023	24	11
2002	23	53	2013	24	2	2024	24	12
2003	23	54	2014	24	3	2025	24	12
2004	23	55	2015	24	4	2026	24	13
2005	23	56	2016	24	5	2027	24	14
2006	23	56	2017	24	6	2028	24	15
2007	23	57	2018	24	6	2029	24	16
2008	23	58	2019	24	7	2030	24	17
2009	23	59	2020	24	8			

This table is calculated to the nearest minute ('). The exact ayanamsha for 1st January 1950 is 23° (degrees) 9.5' (minutes); for 1st January 1975 is 23°30.5'; and for 1st January 2000 it is 23°51.4'. Motion of the ayanamsha for 10 years is 8.38'. For 1 year it is 0.84'. One month is 0.07'.

When purchasing a Sidereal ephemeris, Lahiri's Ephemeris is published annually, or there is a condensed ephemeris for one hundred years (1951 to 2050) calculated for the same *ayanamsha*. Computer programs will give you a choice of *ayanamshas* but always include Lahiri's *Ayanamsha*.

Planetary Rulerships

"The science of astrology treats of the effects of the good or bad deeds (karma) accruing from our previous births." – *Brihat Jataka 1:3*

In Vedic Astrology there are seven principle planets ruling twelve signs. These are tabulated below:

Planet	Sign(s) ruled by Planet
Sun	Leo
Moon	Cancer
Mercury	Gemini, Virgo
Venus	Taurus, Libra
Mars	Aries, Scorpio
Jupiter	Sagittarius, Pisces
Saturn	Capricorn, Aquarius

Sign Rulerships

Each of the 12 signs is associated with one of four elements: fire, earth, air, or water, and with one of three qualities: cardinal, fixed, or mutable. In addition, they alternate between active (day-masculine-extrovert) signs and passive (night-feminine-introverted) signs.

Sign	Active/Passive	Quality	Element
Aries	Active	Cardinal	Fire
Taurus	Passive	Fixed	Earth
Gemini	Active	Mutable	Air
Cancer	Passive	Cardinal	Water
Leo	Active	Fixed	Fire
Virgo	Passive	Mutable	Earth
Libra	Active	Cardinal	Air
Scorpio	Passive	Fixed	Water
Sagittarius	Active	Mutable	Fire
Capricorn	Passive	Cardinal	Earth
Aquarius	Active	Fixed	Air
Pisces	Passive	Mutable	Water

Clarification of terms

Cardinal *(chara)* signs are outgoing and enterprising. Fixed *(sthira)* signs are intense, steadfast and resistant to sudden change. Mutable *(dwiswabhava)* signs are variable and adaptable.

Fire signs are assertive, open and aspiring. Earth signs are practical, steady and grounded. Air signs are sociable and communicative, and water signs are sensitive and instinctive.

To understand the characteristics of each sign it helps to remember (a) its polarity (active/passive), (2) its quality, and (3) its element. Avoid embellishing the sign with other characteristics.

Each of the seven planets will embody the qualities of the sign(s) that it rules.

Abbreviations of the Signs and of the Planets Which Rule Them

Sign	Abbr.	Planet ruling sign	Abbr.
Aries	Ar	Mars	Ma
Taurus	Ta	Venus	Ve
Gemini	Ge	Mercury	Me
Cancer	Cn	Moon	Mo
Leo	Le	Sun	Su
Virgo	Vi	Mercury	Me
Libra	Li	Venus	Ve
Scorpio	Sc	Mars	Ma
Sagittarius	Sg	Jupiter	Ju
Capricorn	Cp	Saturn	Sa
Aquarius	Aq	Saturn	Sa
Pisces	Pi	Jupiter	Ju

The signs represent certain qualities through which the planets have to operate. The manifestation of the planetary energies are conditioned by the characteristic qualities of the signs in which they are placed.

Besides these seven planets there are the two Nodes of the Moon. The North Node of the Moon is known as *Rahu*. The South Node is known as *Ketu*. *Rahu* and *Ketu* are sometimes spoken of as if they were planets although in reality they are invisible points of great potency.

What is the Zodiac?

The zodiac is a broad circular band of the heavens extending about 9 degrees or so on either side of the ecliptic. The ecliptic is the apparent path of the Sun as seen from earth. Within this path of the ecliptic are to be seen the various planets as they journey through the solar system orbiting the Sun.

Symbols of the Planets

Sun	☉
Moon	☽
Mercury	☿
Venus	♀
Mars	♂
Jupiter	♃
Saturn	♄
Uranus	♅
Neptune	♆
Pluto	♇
Rahu	☊
Ketu	☋

Symbols of the Signs

Aries	♈
Taurus	♉
Gemini	♊
Cancer	♋
Leo	♌
Virgo	♍
Libra	♎
Scorpio	♏
Sagittarius	♐
Capricorn	♑
Aquarius	♒
Pisces	♓

The zodiac (and the background of stars that extends 9 degrees on either side) is a circle which is divided into 12 sections, each of these sections constitutes a zodiacal sign measuring 30 degrees of space. As any circle needs to be given a starting point the zodiac circle begins with the sign of Aries; thus 0° Aries is taken as the beginning of the zodiac.

There are other ways of dividing the zodiac. In Vedic astrology it is also divided into 27 stellar constellations known as the Lunar Mansions, Astrims or *Nakshatras*. These too have their initial starting point at 0° Aries, which marks the beginning of *Ashwini*, the first of the *Nakshatras*.

Space is measured in Degrees (°), Minutes (') and Seconds ("). 60 seconds = 1 minute of space and 60 minutes of space = 1 degree of space. Observe the disk of the Moon or the Sun.

The Sun and Moon each cover about half a degree (or 30') of space.

The Twelve Houses

Just as there are 12 signs so there are 12 houses. The 1st house always corresponds to the Ascendant (or Rising Sign), which is the sign that was rising on the eastern horizon at the time of birth. The 12 houses represent different fields of experience and of our environment. They allow the astrologer to pinpoint specific areas of a person's life that will be influenced by each planet.

Order of Planets

In Western astrology it is normal practice to list the planets in order of their distance from the Sun, the exception being the Moon which always follows on from the Sun. Thus: Sun, Moon, Mercury, Venus, Mars, Jupiter, and Saturn.

In Vedic astrology the normal practice is to list the planets in the order of their rulership of the days of the week. The Vedic sequence is shown in the following table:

Day of the Week	Planet
Sunday	Sun
Monday	Moon
Tuesday	Mars
Wednesday	Mercury
Thursday	Jupiter
Friday	Venus
Saturday	Saturn

Birth Chart Diagrams

The Vedic birth chart diagrams differ from the Western wheel type diagram. There are two main chart styles used by Vedic astrologers; one is popular in southern India, the other mainly favoured in the northern, northwestern and central parts of India.

South Indian Chart Diagram

This is the birth chart diagram commonly used in Southern India. Each square (or box) represents a sign, which are always placed as shown below. The box containing the rising sign is always indicated and the planets placed in the box corresponding to the signs in which they are found at the time of birth. This chart gives an instant picture of the signs rather than of the houses. The planets and signs are shown as moving in a clock-wise direction.

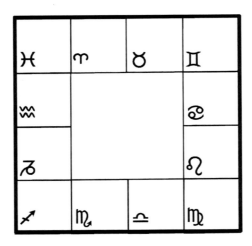

We will be using the North Indian style diagram, which is nearly identical to the birth charts used by western astrologers up until the beginning of the 20th century. The North Indian Chart shows the planets and signs moving in a counterclockwise direction, just as the modern western wheel chart does.

North Indian Chart Diagram

This diagram is commonly found in use in Northern India, and gives a greater visual emphasis on the houses. The Ascendant/1st house always occupies the top central diamond. The houses are then counted in a counterclockwise direction and the symbols of the signs are placed either within the appropriate section or around the outside of the diagram.

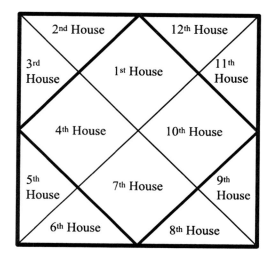

Some astrologers indicate the sign by using its corresponding number—to represent Aries they use the number 1, Taurus would be indicated by 2, Gemini by 3, Cancer 4, Leo 5, Virgo 6, Libra 7, Scorpio 8, Sagittarius 9, Capricorn 10, Aquarius 11, and Pisces 12. In this text the symbols will be used.

In the chart below, the Ascendant/1st house is in Leo. The 2nd house is Virgo. The 3rd house is Libra and contains Mars and Ketu (the South Node of the Moon), The 4th house is in Scorpio and contains the Moon, and so on. The final house is the 12th (upper right hand side of the 1st House). It contains the sign of Cancer and the planet Jupiter.

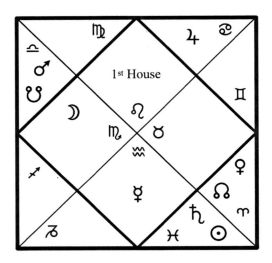

The diagram used for the birth chart, whatever the style used, is known in India as a *Chakra* or *Kundali*. In the West it is called a horoscope, birth chart, radix, or natus.

CHAPTER FOUR

THE PLANETS

"The Moonbeams are also the rays of the Sun." – *Vedas*

Importance of the Sun and Moon

In Western Astrology the Sun is dominant in chart interpretation. In Vedic Astrology the Sun is not *necessarily* regarded as the most important planet. The Sun is a symbol of the spirit-soul *(atma)*. Although of utmost importance, awareness of one's spiritual identity can only be realized, at least during our physical incarnation, by making use of the Sun's light as it is reflected or received by the Moon (symbolizing ego/mind).

We cannot look directly at the brilliance and light of the Sun's disc, but we can gaze steadily at its light as reflected by the Moon. The Moon's role is that of making the radiance and power of the Sun (spirit-soul) manageable, so that we are able to integrate with it during our life on earth. Considering that the deeper and more meaningful side of astrology is all about how we integrate with our true nature and manifest our spiritual destiny during our present life, the Moon is regarded as one of the most significant planets in Jyotish.

Benevolent and Malefic Planets

Certain planets are regarded as beneficial in nature while others are regarded as being essentially malefic (difficult or troublesome). This goes against the grain of modern western astrology, which likes to see good and bad in every planet. While both viewpoints are perfectly valid we will classify the planets as basically benefic or malefic.

This is the method of classification utilized in traditional *Jyotish*. This is no more than a convenient way of dividing them in order to gain further, less polarized insights into their functions.

The benefic planets are Venus and Jupiter. The Moon increases its benefic qualities as it increases its distance from the Sun. It is at its most benefic at Full Moon and at its weakest when conjoined with the Sun at New Moon. An increasing Moon aspected or conjoined with benefics rivals Jupiter in its ability to benefit the birth chart. Mercury is classified as a benefic provided that it is free of the influence of malefic planets. Mercury is highly variable and picks up other planetary influences more easily than any of the other planets.

Mars and Saturn are the main malefics. The Sun is considered to be mildly malefic in nature, as is the Moon when in close proximity to the Sun. Mercury associated with Mars or Saturn easily reflects their qualities. Rahu and Ketu, the two nodes of the Moon, are also considered to be powerful malefics.

Gender

Sun, Mars and Jupiter are considered masculine. Moon and Venus are considered feminine. Mercury and Saturn are considered neutral.

"Male planets are considered stronger when in odd signs, during the fortnight of the waxing Moon and during the daytime. Female planets are considered strong when in even signs, during the fortnight of the waning Moon and at night."
–*Saravali 10:2*

The Nine Planets In Detail

Here we give a basic guide to the meaning and signification's of each of the planets. You can spend a lifetime deepening your understanding of the astrological influences of the planets, as they are foundation stones of any study of astrology.

Sun *(Ravi, Surya)*

The action of the Sun is fortifying and vitalizing. A well placed Sun gives self-reliance, confidence, strength of character, and the ability to inspire others. When weak or afflicted the complexion tends to be pale and energy levels are weak.

The Sun represents the Inner Light or Spirit, consciousness, creative intelligence, aspect of the ego that projects its self onto the outside world, ambition, fame, status in life, power and authority. It also represents one's father. The nature of the Sun is benevolent but firm. When strong it denotes the capacity to organize others and the skill in holding administrative positions, especially in government or politics. The Sun gives a solid body, dignified appearance, and an authoritative tone of voice. It is the main significator for vitality. Well placed it gives a strong constitution, sharp vision and sturdy bones. Yet if it is too dominant or strong it can cause diseases which create heat and high fevers that have a depleting effect on the body.

The Sun owns the sign of Leo. It is exalted in Aries and falls in Libra. Its element is fire.

Moon *(Chandra)*

Just as the Sun represents the positive, self-expressive side of our nature, so the Moon represents the more receptive, feminine, and imaginative side. A strong Moon causes us to be strongly influenced by moods and emotions, to have a good memory or attachment to the past, and to place much importance on the home and family. More than any other planet much depends on the Moon's distance from the Sun and the influence of other planets on it in determining the manner in which it effects us.

The Moon signifies the mother and the mind. The mother nurtures and cares for the child, and is responsible for its formative mental impressions. It indicates our relationship with the mother, and the formative environment of early childhood. The Moon represents the emotional and instinctive side of the mind *(manas)*, the influences, memories and impressions of the past, and how we instinctively express our ego, feelings and emotions.

It is representative of females, the general public and our day to day mode of communicating and interacting with others. Along with Venus it represents feminine qualities and is associated with fertility, the menstrual cycle, conception and birth. The influence of a well placed Moon gives a benevolent and generous nature. The strength or weakness of the Moon reflects the strength or weakness of the mind.

The Moon owns the sign of Cancer. It is exalted in Taurus and falls in Scorpio. Its element is Water.

"The Sun and Moon represent the father and mother respectively of the living beings. In order to predict about the parents one should assess the strengths and weaknesses of these two planets." – *Hora Sara 5.3*

Mercury *(Budha)*

Mercury is the planet of communication, hence it rules over thought, speech, writing, and short journeys. Trade and business activities are also linked to this planet. Well placed it gives a quick and inquiring mind as well as a strong appreciation of logic and rational thought. It can give an exact, matter of fact or critical mentality. In action this planet is quick but variable.

Ruling over the rational conscious mind, Mercury gives intelligence, discrimination, analytical ability, mental flexibility, and humor. It is associated with mathematics, accountancy, and engineering. It denotes trading, business deals, advising and counseling, and astrology. In the birth chart Mercury more than any other planet can easily reflect the qualities of other planets according to influence and association.

A strong Mercury gives a sharp mind, but with a friendly, sociable, and often witty nature. The person tends to appear younger than their actual age and to retain a youthful outlook on life. If overemphasized in the chart one can become mentally restless and overtalkative. Mercury has associations with the skin and nervous system.

The planet Mercury owns the signs of Gemini and Virgo. It is exalted in Virgo (0 to 15 degrees) and falls in Pisces. Its elements are air and earth (especially when in Virgo), which accords with the changeable and mutable nature of the planet.

Venus *(Shukra)*

Being a planet of harmony, balance, and compromise Venus has a strong aversion to discord or conflict. It gives a good appreciation of color, form, and beauty and thus a love of the arts. Venus gives a sociable, friendly, and sympathetic nature, but if badly placed tends to make one lazy, indecisive, and over dependent of others. It is associated with a wide range of emotions, and can give rise to sensuality and self indulgence on the one hand, as well as to a romantic, gentle, and loving nature on the other.

Venus is associated with love, romance, marriage, comforts, luxuries, happiness, wealth, and enjoyment of the good things in life—also conveyances (such as a car or boat), charisma, good taste, passion, eroticism, and sexual pleasures. It represents the marriage partner in a man's horoscope. It can signify a vocation in the fields of finance, fashion, beauty, or the arts. Venus rules music, sensuality and items of luxury, color, and fragrance.

When strong, Venus makes one fertile and attractive. It gives charm and beauty to the features, a well-proportioned body, and large eyes. If too strong it can give excessive sensuality or a strongly effeminate nature.

Venus owns the signs of Taurus and Libra. It is exalted in Pisces and falls in Virgo. Its elements are Water (especially when in Pisces) and Air (especially when in Libra).

Mars *(Kuja, Mangal)*

The nature of Mars is quick, decisive, and restless. It loves to have the freedom to act independently and will stand firm when challenged. This is the planet that gives us drive, courage, and initiative. Badly placed it can give rise to argument, disputes, aggression, and violence. There is not a lot of refinement or subtlety about Mars—it likes to be direct, assertive, and outspoken.

Mars signifies energy, potency, action, and motivation. It is associated with technical or mechanical ability, sports, competitive attitudes, accidents, fires, weapons, sexual potency, physical strength, and surgical operations. It also represents younger brothers and sisters. When its influence dominates the Ascendant it gives short stature, a well-built body, and a ruddy complexion.

A strong Mars can incline one to a career in military and police forces, or to vocations involving fire, metals, engineering, or chemicals. It is also associated with surgery and dentistry. Although the influence of Mars can make one willful, harsh and unyielding, or active, openhearted and generous, a weak Mars causes one to lack courage, determination, and will power.

Mars owns the signs of Aries and Scorpio. It is exalted in Capricorn and falls in Cancer. The element of Mars is Fire.

Jupiter *(Guru, Brihaspati)*

Like the Sun and Mars, Jupiter is a planet associated with the fire element, but in this case it is the fire of the mental and spiritual planes. It can give an attraction to philosophical and religious thought, spiritual interests, and a love of freedom, but freedom that is tempered with compassion and justice.

It rules wisdom gained through experience and as such is the planet of teaching, counseling, and higher learning. Professions such as teaching, law, and theology are associated with this planet. It can incline one towards holding political or administrative positions. Well placed it brings good fortune, great optimism, and a natural faith and trust in the goodness and abundance of the Universe or Spiritual Reality.

Its link to Sagittarius gives a fondness for animals and of open air sports and recreation. It will also give a broadminded outlook and generous nature capable of bestowing intelligence, wisdom, and spiritual knowledge. Badly placed it causes one to trust too much in lucky breaks and opportunities, to exaggerate, become overoptimistic, overindulgent, to gamble or to take excessive risks.

Jupiter can give a shade of gold to the iris of the eye, and bestows a golden complexion, an impressive disposition, and a large body, especially when ruling or aspecting the Ascendant or influencing the Ascendant lord (planet ruling the Ascendant sign).

Expansion, creativity, religion, ritual, spiritual growth, meditation, compassion, morality, legal affairs, good fortune, luck, speculation, gambling, and foreign travels are all ruled by Jupiter. It is also representative of the guru or spiritual teacher, and is associated with spiritual insight and divine grace. It is the significator of children, elder brothers, and of the marriage partner in a female horoscope.

Jupiter owns the signs of Sagittarius and Pisces. It is exalted in Cancer and falls in Capricorn. The element of Jupiter is Ether *(Akash)*.

"In completely warding off evil and in promoting auspicious results, Jupiter is the most powerful of all the planets." – *Phaldeepika 4.11*

"The Sun, Saturn, Mars, waning Moon, Rahu and Ketu are cruel."
– *Brihat Parasara Hora Shastra 3.11*

Saturn *(Shani)*

Saturn is recognized as the planet of restriction, sorrow, and limitation. It can make one fearful, pessimistic, and despondent. A strong Saturn gives a strong belief in the work ethic, and makes one careful, cautious, and practical. It contrasts much with the buoyant optimism of Jupiter. Saturn tends to believe in and trust solid material realities rather than in luck or God. However, Saturn can also give a detachment from sensual life and from one's material possessions. As such it is often found well placed in the charts of spiritually evolved people—typical is the *sanyasi,* one who lives in the world without any material attachments or possessions.

Positively, Saturn gives determination, ambition, patience and the ability to structure and organize our lives. Without its presence in the chart there would be no boundaries in which to contain and organize the outgoing and expansive energies of Jupiter.

Saturn is said to lack ambition. He survives yet does not thrive. Motivation comes in the way of overcoming struggle, and not by an inspirational desire to acheive something great. Saturn can show our weaknesses and liabilities, and a strong Saturn can help us endure in spite of those short comings.

Saturn signifies the passage of time and gains in strength, power and emphasis as we grow older. In its role as Old Father Time it rules old age and longevity. It is a planet that we tend to "grow into"—to feel more comfortable with as we mature in wisdom and experience.

The negative side of Saturn is associated with fear, reservation, restriction, adversity, delays, loss, misery, melancholia, and depression.

Saturn represents authority figures and authoritative institutions (such as government), leadership abilities, spiritual growth, nonattachment, asceticism, perfection, material values, concentration, hard work, sense of duty and responsibility, structural matters, construction work, theft, and to matters relating to the earth such as farming, archaeology, and mining. It also signifies jobs requiring a lot of hard work, often with little remuneration. As it can produce feelings of insecurity there is often an instinct to conserve or to be miserly. A badly placed Saturn can also make one selfish and indolent.

If Saturn is very prominent in the chart it can give a skinny body, tall stature, a somewhat dark complexion, and prominent veins. It can also give a somewhat slow and melancholic nature. Saturn owns the signs of Capricorn and Aquarius. It is exalted in Libra and falls in Aries. Saturn's main element is air (especially when in Libra) with earth as a secondary influence.

North and South Nodes of the Moon *(Rahu and Ketu)*

The energy of Rahu (North Node) is directed outward, found dominant in the charts of extrovert film stars, politicians, and of others who seek public acclaim. The energy of Ketu (South Node) is directed inwards, found dominant in introvert types, particularly renunciates such as monks, nuns, sadhus, and yogis. Both nodes possess an instinctive, compulsive, and obsessive side to their nature.

"Rahu has a smoke blue like body, lives in forests and is horrible. He is windy in temperament and he is intelligent. Ketu is like Rahu."
– *Brihat Parasara Hora Shastra 3.30*

Rahu

Rahu is said to behave somewhat like Saturn. Rahu indicates diplomatic jobs, jobs requiring the manipulation of facts, and dealings that involve poisons or drugs. It signifies cheaters, pleasure seekers, and insincere and immoral acts. Rahu can cause us to push our selves to the limits in order to fulfill our desires and ambitions.

Rahu carries an energy of worldly desire and represents, according to its placement in the chart, how and where our desires *(kama)* are most easily converted into deeds *(karma)*. Rahu, the Dragon's Head, is associated with the power of the mind separated from the heart energy (compassion) and thus easily leads us into worldly illusion. It is associated with the descent of spirit into matter and the dulling of higher consciousness through association with materialism. In the right measure the energy of Rahu can lead us to worldly accomplishments, but if overemphasized it can create insatiable desires.

Rahu's element is Air (secondary; earth); it's element is easily modified by that of any planet which conjoins or aspects it.

Ketu

Ketu is said to behave somewhat like Mars. Ketu has association with mass catastrophes and wars. It represents psychic forces residing in the subconscious that can cause compulsive forms of behavior. It is associated with invisible forces, viruses and epidemic diseases.

Ketu also has the ability to act as an agent of spiritual rebirth and regeneration. At its best Ketu can bestow wisdom, discrimination and nonattachment to worldly desires. It is known as *moksha karaka* (representative or bestower of enlightenment) and *gyana karaka* (representative of wisdom). It has the potential to be the most spiritual energy of the birth chart, being associated with the evolution and refinement of consciousness. When we turn inward and seek to regain our original state of enlightened consciousness the energy of Ketu is capable of leading us out of the maze of material illusion an freeing us of our delusions.

However, for the materially minded person Ketu is capable of being a dark, destructive, and disruptive influence.

Ketu's element is Fire (secondary; Air), but, as with Rahu, judge this also by planets that influence it.

In the classical Jyotish texts there are differences of opinion regarding the ownership, exaltation, and fall of the Nodes. Often there is no reference to their sign associations These differences also occur in present day books by both Western and Indian authors.

There is general agreement that the Nodes do well in the signs owned by Mercury, Gemini, and Virgo. Rahu does well in the signs of Saturn, Capricorn, and Aquarius, while Ketu does well in the signs of Mars, Aries and Scorpio.

According to the 19th century jyotishi Ramadayaiu:

"Rahu's exaltation sign is Gemini and Virgo is his own sign, while Ketu's exaltation sign is Sagittarius and Pisces is his own sign. But according to some Scorpio is the exaltation sign of Rahu and Aquarius that of Ketu."
– *Sanketnadhi 1:30*

However, most classical authors ascribe the exaltation of Rahu to Taurus and the exaltation of Ketu to Scorpio. This is more logical as Rahu is described as being similar to Saturn (which is compatible with Venus— therefore is happy in Taurus) and Ketu is considered similar to Mars (which rules Scorpio). Perhaps the differences arise because the Nodes always aspect each other due to being in exact opposition, so their energies easily become interchanged. These differences also arise due to the very subtle and variable nature of the Nodes. Every astrologer will vary a little in their understanding of them, hence the differences of opinion.

The signs of Jupiter (Sagittarius and Pisces) help to uplift and spiritualize their energies, particularly those of Ketu. The signs of Venus tend to bring out their more worldly and sensual side, particularly Rahu's.

Neither of the Nodes are happy in the signs of Cancer or Leo, owned as they are by the Sun and Moon, great enemies of the Nodes.

In order to better understand the Nodes one should study the story of their origin, as told in spiritual classics such as the *Bhagavat Purana*. This tells of a time prior to the present material creation when the gods and demons (spiritualizing and materializing forces) cooperated with each other for the purpose of churning the Milk Ocean (galactic substance) in order to create certain treasures. They were assisted in this process by Lord Vishnu, who distributed Amrita—one of the treasures that had emanated from the ocean.

Amrita was a nectarian drink that produced immortality. This nectar was only intended for the gods. The demons had their own drink, an intoxicating substance known as Varuni. One of the demons, however, by his cunning was able to sit with the gods, between the Sun and the Moon. The demon quickly sipped a share of the nectar before being discovered. Lord Vishnu quickly decapitated the demon. The head became Rahu and the body (tail) became Ketu. And there they are today, behaving exactly like two parts of a demon: dark, invisible, and chaotic forces, one minus a heart (feeling) and the other minus a head (logic), eternally eclipsing the Sun and Moon. This is why an eclipse of the Sun or the Moon is considered such an ill omen —for a short period of time the light of the Sun or the Moon is overcome by the darkness of one of the Nodes.

CHAPTER FIVE

PLANETARY CONDITIONS

The Fivefold Relationship Between Planets
(Panchadha maitri)

Any planet can have one of five types of relationship with any other planet by combining two sets of relationships: Permanent, which is always applicable, and Temporary, which is only applicable to an individual birth chart.

1. Permanent Relationships – (Rahu and Ketu are not included in the above classification.)

Planet	Friends	Neutrals	Enemies
Sun	Moon, Mars, Jupiter	Mercury	Venus, Saturn
Moon	Sun, Mercury	Mars, Jupiter, Venus, Saturn	
Mercury	Sun, Venus	Mars, Jupiter, Saturn	Moon
Venus	Mercury, Saturn	Mars, Jupiter	Sun, Moon
Mars	Sun, Moon, Jupiter	Venus, Saturn	Mercury
Jupiter	Sun, Moon, Mars	Saturn.	Mercury, Venus
Saturn	Mercury, Venus	Jupiter	Sun. Moon, Mars

These relationships are called permanent because they always apply, regardless of a planet's relationship to any other planet in an individual chart. In contrast, the varying position of planets to each other in an individual birth chart gives rise to a set of temporary relationships.

2. Temporal Relationships – Planets that are in the 2nd, 3rd, 4th, 10th, 11th, or 12th sign as counted from the planet under consideration become Temporary Friends. Planets in the *same sign*, or in 5th, 6th, 7th, 8th, or 9th as counted from the planet under consideration are considered Temporary Enemies.

Thus each planet in the birth chart has a Permanent *and* a Temporary relationship with every other planet in the chart.

Let us look at the birth chart of Albert Einstein.

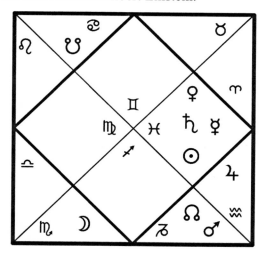

Suppose we wish to find the permanent and temporary relationship between the Sun and the Moon. By referring to the table of Permanent Relationships we find that the Sun is a friend to the Moon, but if we count the signs from the Sun to the Moon we find that the Moon, being 9th from the Sun, becomes a temporary enemy of the Sun. If we look at the relationship between Jupiter and the Sun we find that the Sun is a permanent friend of Jupiter. Being placed in the 2nd sign from Jupiter it is also a temporary friend.

The various combinations of permanent and temporary relationship give rise to five types of planetary relationship:

A permanent enemy, which is also a temporary enemy, becomes a <u>Great Enemy</u>.
A permanent neutral, which is temporary enemy, becomes an <u>Enemy</u>.
A permanent enemy, which is a temporary friend, becomes a <u>Neutral</u>, as does a permanent friend and temporary enemy.
A permanent neutral, which is a temporary friend, becomes a <u>Friend</u>.
A permanent friend, which is also a temporary friend becomes a <u>Great Friend</u>.

> Friend + Friend = Great Friend
> Neutral + Friend = Friend
> Friend + Enemy = Neutral
> Neutral + Enemy = Enemy
> Enemy + Enemy = Great Enemy

This information will be used to judge many chart factors involving the planets. For example, if we wanted to find out if the quality of the sign placement of planets in Einstein's chart we can note the following:

Sun is in a great friends sign (friend + friend) = very good results.
Moon is in its fall = poor results (For exaltations and falls see next chapter.)
Mars is exalted = excellent results.
Mercury is in the sign of a friend (neutral + friend) =good results.
Jupiter is in a friends sign (neutral + friend) = good results.
Venus is exalted =excellent results.
Saturn is in a friend's sign (neutral + friend) = good results.

These fivefold relationships can also be used to assist in the assessment of planetary aspects and planetary time periods.

Combustion *(Asta)*

"Planets become weak if eclipsed by the Sun. Such weak planets do not give good results in respect to the *bhavas* [houses], *yogas* and *dashas* that they are connected with." – *Saravali 3:36*

A planet is said to be combust when it appears to be too close to the Sun. Such an occurrence is considered damaging to the influence of the planet concerned, although it should be remembered that Mercury and Venus are never found very far away from the Sun. Generally these two planets need to be within a few degrees of an exact conjunction with the Sun to be considered seriously harmed by combustion.

Combust planets mainly weaken or harm the houses that they rule. For example, if we have an Aries ascendant with a combust Venus (ruler of the 7th house), relationships may suffer. The following results relate to the house rulership of combust planets.

- The 1st lord combust can weaken health.
- The 2nd lord combust can weaken family ties.
- The 3rd lord combust is difficult for younger siblings.
- The 4th lord combust causes the mother to suffer.
- The 5th lord combust gives trouble with children or difficulty having them.
- The 6th lord combust gives troubles with subordinates, or weakens our immunity and resistance to disease.
- The 7th lord combust gives problems in relationship and marriage.
- The 8th lord combust weakens longevity.
- The 9th lord combust is harmful for the father.
- The 10th lord combust creates difficult relationships with those in authority.
- The 11th lord combust is difficult for elder siblings.
- The 12th lord combust causes one to experience feelings of loss and isolation.

Other factors must combine with these indications for them to be significant. Combust planets mainly effect our relationships with others, or our own levels of health or vitality. It does not seem to seriously impair such house significations as wealth, career, intelligence or spirituality.

On average the orbs of combustion are as follows:

- Moon 12 to 15 degrees
- Mercury 2 to 14 degrees
- Venus 4 to 10 degrees
- Mars 8 to 17 degrees
- Jupiter 8 to 11 degrees
- Saturn 8 to 15 degrees

The astrologer James Braha suggests that all planets within an 8 degree orb of the Sun become combust. When the larger orbs are used combustion is not always counted as an important factor. David Frawley, a widely respected Vedic Astrologer, suggests using the smaller orbs. Obviously the closer a planet is to the Sun the more noticeable would be the results—a planet within a few degrees of an exact conjunction with the Sun would be truly combust.

One point worth bearing in mind is that combustion is much more severe if the Sun becomes the ruler of a difficult house. For example, this would occur if Capricorn were the sign on the Ascendant, because, through Leo, the Sun would rule the difficult 8th house, thus becoming more malefic in nature. In this case combust planets would be more severely afflicted than if, for example, the Sun ruled the benefic 9th house (which would be the case for someone with a Sagittarius Ascendant).

Here is a typical example of combustion:

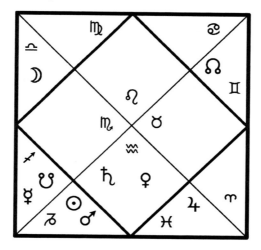

Mars is combust with the Sun (3 degrees apart). Mars rules the 4th and 9th houses. The 4th is the house of the home and mother and the 9th rules the father. Although Mars gives this person great determination and energy she had an unhappy childhood, her father was an alcoholic and her relationship with her mother was so difficult that they have not spoken to each other for many years. Mars is exalted in Capricorn and in other areas of her life this planet has played a positive role.

Retrograde Planets *(Vakra)*

When reference is made to a retrograde planet we are referring to a visual phenomenon that occurs due to different speeds of the planets in relation to the earth. When this happens to a planet, its speed decreases until it appears to become stationary. It will then appear to be moving backwards (retrograde) through the zodiac for a period of time. Then it will appear to gradually slow down, become stationary, and then resume forward motion again. Only the Lunar Nodes maintain a regular retrograde movement. The Sun and Moon are never retrograde. In chart data the letter R is used to indicate retrograde motion.

The most important point to remember when dealing with a retrograde planet is that the energies that it represents will manifest in a more *internalized* manner. From a material and practical point of view this has disadvantages in that it causes a person to express those energies in a more reserved, perhaps less confident manner. However from a spiritual point of view this deepening and internalizing effect can have its benefits.

Three or more retrograde planets in a horoscope indicate a person of a critical nature or a tendency towards negative thinking or negative responses.

Mercury and Venus are less affected by being retrograde. Their retrograde motion is of two kinds. They can retrograde towards the Sun, thus moving towards becoming combust. This is more difficult. Or they can retrograde away from the Sun, which is less difficult.

It is not good to have a retrograde planet afflicted by other negative factors in the horoscope. If this happens then the results of retrograde motion becomes more difficult to deal with.

Malefics (Mars and Saturn) when retrograde may cause harm, particularly when they are located in angles. This increases their tendency to cause delays, obstructions, and limitations.

Benefics (Venus and Jupiter) when retrograde tend to become weak and unreliable in their ability to help us on a practical level, losing much of their positive warmth and energy.

By itself a planet being retrograde is a fairly minor factor and should not be allowed to outweigh more important factors such as the aspects of other planets or disposition by sign or house position.

Any planet that is retrograde in the birth chart tends to be more strongly associated with karmic influences and the function the planet represents will have strong past life connections. *Mercury* retrograde will show a mind taken over by the influences of the past or having an insight into the past. This may cause hesitation in speech or speech defects, if afflicted, but if well placed will give a good knowledge of history. *Mars* retrograde may show violent or impulsive influences carried over from past lives, which may result in injury.

Each retrograde planet should be examined according to its natural and temporal status to see what karmic forces or processes it may be projecting. These will manifest during the period and sub-period of the planet, or during its transits around the chart.

Past karma also tends to work itself out during the retrograde transits of planets. Retrograde planets make us deal with unresolved issues from the past. Malefics will make us experience negative effects of past karma; benefics help us clear the influences of the past so that we can move forward in life. Many retrograde planets in the birth chart show the need for clearing out karma or for ending a cycle of karmic experience. Few or no retrograde planets in the chart show the beginning of a new cycle of karma.

In medical astrology a retrograde planet ruling houses which relate to one's health are found to be damaging in regard to vitality and recuperative abilities.

CHAPTER SIX

PLANETS AND SIGNS

"...The Sun is the soul, the Moon is the mind, Mars is strength, Mercury is speech, Jupiter is knowledge and happiness, Venus is desire, and Saturn is sorrow." – *Brihat Jataka 2:1*

The following table shows the signs and the planets which rule them. Notice that each planet rules two signs except for the Sun and Moon which rule only one sign each.

SIGN	PLANET
Aries	Mars
Taurus	Venus
Gemini	Mercury
Cancer	Moon
Leo	Sun
Virgo	Mercury
Libra	Venus
Scorpio	Mars
Sagittarius	Jupiter
Capricorn	Saturn
Aquarius	Saturn
Pisces	Jupiter

Exaltation and Fall of Planets

In the previous chapter on the planets there is reference to the sign(s) which the planet owns, as well as to their sign of exaltation and fall.

Planet	Rules	Exalted	Moolatrikona	Fall
Sun	Leo	Aries	Leo	Libra
Moon	Cancer	Taurus	Cancer	Scorpio
Mercury	Gemini & Virgo	Virgo	Virgo	Pisces
Venus	Taurus & Libra	Pisces	Libra	Virgo
Mars	Aries & Scorpio	Capricorn	Aries	Cancer
Jupiter	Sagittarius & Pisces	Cancer	Sagittarius	Capricorn
Saturn	Capricorn & Aquarius	Libra	Aquarius	Aries

Planet	Exalted (Uucha)	Moolatrikona	Fall (Neecha)
Sun	Aries	Leo (0 to 20)	Libra
Moon	Taurus (0 to 3)	Cancer (0 to 3)	Scorpio (0 to 3)
Mercury	Virgo (0 to 15)	Virgo (16 to 20)	Pisces (0 to 15)
Venus	Pisces	Libra (0 to 20)	Virgo
Mars	Capricorn	Aries (0 to 12)	Cancer
Jupiter	Cancer	Sagittarius (0 to 5)	Capricorn
Saturn	Libra	Aquarius (0 to 20)	Aries

Remember that a planet in its own sign expresses its essential nature with ease and confidence, benefiting the house that it occupies as well as the houses that it owns. When found placed in its sign of exaltation *(uucha)* it expresses itself with great strength and intensity, although whether for good or bad will depend on other factors associated with the planet. The sign directly opposite to its exaltation sign is that of the planets "fall." In the sign of its fall *(neecha)* it becomes weak and lacks the ability to do much good. Although debilitated it may still give troublesome and difficult results, particularly if it happens to be Mars or Saturn.

Moolatrikona

In Vedic astrology you will find frequent references not only to the quality and strength of a planet based on its ownership, exaltation or fall, but also to its *moolatrikona* position, another factor determined by the planet's sign placement. A planet in *moolatrikona* (*moola* = root, and *trikona* = triangle) is considered stronger than when its own sign but not quite so elevated or as powerful as when in its exaltation.

Each planet "rules" two signs, yet each planet, although it has rulership of both signs, has only partial "ownership" of one of its signs (with the exception of the Sun and Moon which rule one sign each). The following table gives the *swakshetra* or areas of ownership.

Planet	Degree extent of ownership
Sun	20 to 30 of Leo
Moon	3 to 30 of Cancer
Mercury	All of Gemini and 20 to 30 of Virgo
Venus	All of Taurus and 20 to 30 of Libra
Mars	20 to 30 of Aries and all of Scorpio
Jupiter	5 to 30 of Sagittarius and all of Pisces
Saturn	All of Capricorn and 20 to 30 of Aquarius

Within each exaltation sign there is a degree of greatest exaltation, and 180 degrees away, in the opposite sign will be found the degree of its maximum fall. These are as follows:

Planet	Exaltation Degree	Degree of Fall
Sun	10 Aries	10 Libra
Moon	3 Taurus	3 Scorpio
Mercury	15 Virgo	15 Pisces
Venus	27 Pisces	27 Virgo
Mars	28 Capricorn	28 Cancer
Jupiter	5 Cancer	5 Capricorn
Saturn	20 Libra	20 Aries

"In the case of a planet owning two houses, that house which happens to be the Moolatrikona one will predominate and its effects alone will be felt in full while the effects of its other house will be half."

– Phaldeepika 15:11

The above verse from Mantreshwara's 15th century masterpiece *Phaldeepika* describes an important use of *Moolatrikona* signs. As an example, if we take the birth chart of Margaret Thatcher we find that Saturn rules both her 4th house (home and domestic life) and her 5th (creative intelligence). (Thatcher's chart is on the following page.)

As Saturn is very favorably placed in its exaltation sign of Libra it is worth considering which of the two houses will be most emphasized. As Aquarius is Saturn's *moolatrikona* sign we can appreciate that the 5th house is going to be the most emphasized.

With the exception of the Moon and Mercury, all of the *moolatrikona* signs are the positive day signs (fire or air) owned by the each planet i.e. Sun = Leo, Mars = Aries, Venus = Libra, Jupiter = Sagittarius, and Saturn = Aquarius. The reasons for the two exceptions are that the Moon does not own a positive (fire or air) sign and in the case of Mercury its positive sign Gemini is too mutable and airy by nature to produce the consistency and strength needed for a moolatrikona sign.

Margaret Thatcher's Chart

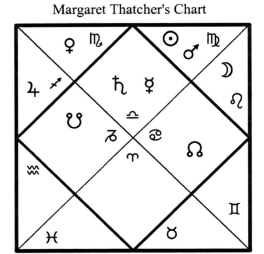

If a planet owns two signs, and falls in a difficult house (such as the 6th,8th or 12th) and the other in a beneficial house, the planet will incline towards giving the results of the house in which its *Moolatrikona* sign falls. For example, a Virgo ascendant has the 5th and 6th houses ruled by Saturn since Capricorn owns the 5th house and Aquarius owns the 6th. Thus Saturn will give more prominent results in relation to 6th house affairs (health, disease, service to others etc.). If Saturn is afflicted there are likely to be health problems, although if well placed this may manifest as an interest in health or healing techniques. In the case of an Aries ascendant Jupiter would own the 9th house (Sagittarius) and the 12th house (Pisces). Jupiter would be favorable due to its ownership of the 9th despite its ownership of the 12th due to Sagittarius being its *moolatrikona* sign.

Strength of Planets Due to Sign Placement

Although it is not a particularly good practice when judging a birth chart to view everything too mathematically by reducing the factors involved to points and percentages of strength or benevolence, this approach can sometimes be helpful in assessing the various planetary factors involved.

The following gives a perspective on the degree to which a planet will manifest its essential nature due to sign placement. However this will be modified by such things as aspect and house placement.

- A planet in its fall gives up to 12.5%
- A planet in an enemy sign gives up to 25%
- A planet in a neutral sign gives up to 37.5%
- A planet in a friends sign gives up to 50%
- A planet in its own negative sign gives up to 62.5%
- A planet in its own positive sign gives up to 75%
- A planet in *moolatrikona* gives up to 87.5%
- An exalted planet gives up to 100%

Sanskrit Names of the Planets and Signs

There are several Sanskrit names for the various planets. We list the most commonly used ones, but will continue to use the familiar English names.

Planet	Sanskrit Names
Sun	Surya, Ravi
Moon	Chandra, Soma
Mars	Kuja, Mangala
Mercury	Buddha
Jupiter	Guru, Brihaspati
Venus	Shukra
Saturn	Shani
North Node	Rahu
South Node	Ketu

The Sanskrit term for a planet is *graha*. Graha means that which attracts, grasps or seizes hold. In fact this is what the planetary energies do to us.

The planets grab hold of us and control us, causing us to react and to behave in certain ways. The *grahas* are the astral vehicles which channel karmic forces stored in our causal body, and thus direct the course of our lives.

The Sanskrit terms for a sign of the zodiac is a *rashi*, meaning a group, heap or cluster (of stars). The familiar birth chart which divides the circle of the zodiac into twelve, each consisting of 30 degrees, is known as the *Rashi* chart. This distinguishes it from a variety of other charts (division charts) which divide the zodiac in to segments ranging from 15 degrees to half a degree of space.

Shirshodaya and *Prishtodaya* Signs

The signs are divided into two groups; those said to be "front-rising" *(shirshodaya),* and those said to be "back-rising" *(prishtodaya).* The *shirshodaya* signs are considered to be more auspicious than the back -rising, *prishtodaya* signs.

The Sanskrit names of the 12 signs are as follows:

Sign of the Zodiac	Sanskrit Name
Aries	Mesha
Taurus	Vrisha
Gemini	Mithuna
Cancer	Karkata
Leo	Simha
Virgo	Kanyaa
Libra	Tulaa
Scorpio	Vrishchika
Sagittarius	Dhanhu
Capricorn	Makara
Aquarius	Kumbha
Pisces	Meena

- The front-rising or *shirshodaya* signs are Gemini, Virgo, Leo, Libra, Scorpio and Aquarius.
- The back-rising or *prishtodaya* signs are Aries, Taurus, Cancer, Sagittarius and Capricorn.
- Pisces is said to have the characteristics of both so is known as "both-ways rising" or *ubhayodaya*.

When natural benefics (Jupiter, Venus, waxing Moon or Mercury free from the influence of malefic planets) occupy a *shirshodaya* sign they increase there ability to do good, while natural malefics (Mars, Saturn, waning Moon or Mercury associated with malefics) in a *prishtodaya* sign increase their ability to do harm. While occupying *shirshodaya* signs they are less malefic. Conversely benefics occupying *prishtodaya* signs are less benefic.

The *shirshodaya* and *prishtodaya* sign influences are not to be given *too* much emphasis but used to give a finer shade of interpretation. Their influence is a little more important when determining the malefic/benefic nature of planets in the rising sign.

Another use of this sign classification is given in the following quotation:

"A planet in a Shirshodaya sign yields its results at the initial portion of the period of life influenced by it. But the same planet in a Prishtodaya sign does it in the final stage. If the planet should be in a sign that has both characteristics it becomes fruitful at all times."

– Jataka Parajataka 2:86

The planets are also classified as *shirshodaya* and *prishtodaya*. The Moon, Mercury and Venus are *shirshodaya* (front-rising), while Jupiter (in keeping with its rulership of Pisces) rises both ways. The Sun, Mars, Saturn and the Nodes are *prishtodaya* (back-rising).

Gandanta

Any planet found in the very beginning or end of a sign (0° or 29°) is considered to be weakened by being placed, at the nodal point, or junction point *(sandhi)* of two signs. If the junction point occurs between a water and a fire sign this is considered to be particularly inauspicious and is referred to as *gandanta*. The reason is that the junction between water and fire signs is also a junction point between two Nakshatras. The 27 Nakshatras or Lunar Mansions, each measuring 13°20', will be explained in a later chapter. Any planet between 26°40' of a water sign and 3°20' is considered to be in a *gandanta* area of the zodiac, and therefore weakened. The closer the planet happens to be to the exact conjunction point of the two signs the weaker it becomes.

Strength of the Moon

There has been reference to the Moon being either benefic or malefic. This variation of condition does not necessarily require the association of the Moon with a benefic or malefic planet. It very much depends on the relationship of the Moon to the Sun. When the moon is waxing (moving away from the Sun) it gains in strength and increases its benefic qualities. At Full Moon it is exactly opposite the Sun and has reached its greatest point of increase and at that time is at its strongest and most benevolent. When waning (moving towards the Sun) it decreases in strength and loses its power to do good, until it conjoins with the Sun (New Moon). From a materialistic point of view it is not good to have the Moon too close to the Sun although from a spiritual perspective this represents the submission of the mind and lower self (Moon) to the Atma or Spiritual Self (Sun).

In astrology the month is divided into two fortnights—the bright half of the month *(shukla paksha),* when the Moon is waxing, and the dark half of the month *(krishna paksha)* when the Moon is waning. The variation in lunar strength is thus dependent on the lunar cycle as the Moon increases in strength from New Moon to Full Moon and decreases in strength as it returns to New Moon. This changing cycle of the Moon's strength is known as *paksha bala.*

Paksha bala gradually increases and decreases over the moon's nightly course of the lunar month, yet for practical purposes the Moon is considered weak by some astrologers if its distance from the Sun is less than 90 degrees. If the Moon's distance is greater than 120 degrees from the Sun it is considered very good. Another way of viewing *paksha bala* is expressed in the following verse:

"Judgement should be given after examining the strength of the Moon. During the first ten days of the lunar month the Moon is of moderate strength. During the middle period of ten days, its strength is full. During the third portion of ten days, its strength is on the wane and its effectiveness also will steadily decline." *–Phaldeepika 19:8*

CHAPTER SEVEN

THE HOUSES

"A planet produces the full effect of the house in which it is situated when its degree in the sign it occupies is the same as the degree occupied by the Ascendant point of the Rising Sign." – *Phaldeepika 8:34*

Extent of Each House

The extent of each house is 30 degrees. The strength of the results given by a planet is analyzed on the basis of its placement in a particular house. The degree rising on the horizon at the time of birth is considered as the most effective point of the ascendant and similarly the same degree would be considered as the most effective point of each house. Suppose the ascending degree is 12 degree of Virgo. This becomes the most sensitive and effective point of the 1st house. The most sensitive and effective point of every other house would also be the 12th degree of whatever sign the house occupies. The planets placed in a house on or near this point has maximum impact on the concerns of that house.

Meanings Of The Twelve Houses

The indications of each house are built up in stages, starting with a few keywords and brief sentences, followed by a more detailed description. The *Karaka* planets are those planets that should be studied in order to gain additional insights regarding a particular house.

All departments of one's life are covered by the 12 houses and the list of attributes for each house could easily be greatly extended. However, it is more important that you understand the scope and spirit of each house. Familiarize yourself with the keywords and short sentences.

When these have been absorbed, study the more detailed description. Proceed slowly, trying to absorb the "feel" of each house. This is more important than trying to learn the signification of each house by rote.

THE FIRST HOUSE

The 1st House *(Lagna bhava)* has an affinity with Aries and Mars.

Key Words: The body; self-projection.

Relates to the body, especially the head, also to the ego and self awareness.

The 1st House is associated with the ability to project one's personality into the outside world. It is strongly related to the personal appearance, and in particular to the head. A strong first house gives alertness and a strong sense of self-awareness. Planets placed in this house play an important role in the development of one's personal character and have a significant role to play in the interpretation of the chart. The individual identifies strongly with them for good or ill. This house is also associated with one's health, strength, and vitality. It is the main factor for determining the physical constitution but more generally shows our orientation to life as a whole.

For any significant accomplishment in life a strong 1st house, along with a strong ruling planet, is necessary. Through the 1st house, the influences of other planets are able to manifest their qualities through our personality and become an integral part of our lives. The Ascendant/1st house acts as our link to the outside world and is the most important factor in the chart. The strength or weakness of the Ascendant is capable of overriding all other factors, and if we correctly interpret all the factors pertaining to the Ascendant we have established the essential features of the person's life—a summary of the complete horoscope. A favorable 1st house can neutralize many of the problems that may exist in other areas of the horoscope.

Specific Indications: The personal self. Physical appearance, complexion, body, face, head. Personality, character, disposition, general tendencies, conduct. Overall well-being, health and happiness. Longevity, vitality, strength and will power. Dignity, self-esteem, self-love, confidence. Status, fame, ability to be recognized, general prosperity. Birth, early childhood, start in life. General disposition in life.

Karaka planet for 1st house: the Sun.

Type of house: The 1st house is a *kona* (angular) house.

THE SECOND HOUSE

The 2nd House *(Dhana Bhava)* has an affinity to Taurus and Venus.

Key Words: Values; Wealth.

Relates to the gathering and holding of personal and material resources.

The 2nd House is related to the exploration of material aspects of the physical world. Planets placed here are associated with our personal assets and sense of self-worth. This house is very much connected with finances and personal income, and to those skills which are directly related to our ability to provide for ourselves in life.

Difficult planetary placements in this house undermine the feeling of self-worth and create fixations as regards the need for security—particularly financial security. Vedic astrology also relates speech, truthfulness, early family life, the period of childhood, education and imagination to the 2nd house.

This house corresponds to the facial features . Related to the mouth it shows our appetite and may indicate taste (food preferences). As the house of speech it shows the capacity for speech and communication.

Specific Indications: Money, wealth, possessions, finances. Values. Speech (tone of voice, use of bad language, speech defects etc.). Orators, poets. Imagination. Truthfulness, Early family life and education. Face, neck, and throat. Mouth, taste, tongue, the food one eats. Vision in general, right eye in particular. Charity. Dress. Gems and Jewelry.

Karaka planet: Jupiter.

Type of house: The second house is *maraka* (killer) house, but is otherwise neutral in nature.

THE THIRD HOUSE

The 3rd House *(Bratru Bhava)* has an affinity with Gemini and Mercury.

Key Word: Mental qualities.

Governs mentality, curiosity and research.

The 3rd House describes mental abilities and experiences associated with learning and communication. Brothers and sisters are shown here, as well as our early school years. The 3rd house is also connected with the surroundings of our immediate environment—neighbors, friends and companions, as well as with facilities for travel and communication (cars, trains, bicycles, letters, and telephones).

Vedic astrology also associates this house with our desires, and with such qualities as courage and bravery; also the fine arts, music, dance and drama. It shows our motivation and indicates our main interests and talents, whether physical or mental— what we really like to do. It also shows less important interests, sports and hobbies. Well-placed planets here can give a capacity for profound interest, deep research and scientific thinking.

This is also a house of prowess, and is symbolized by the arms.

It shows our basic energy in life, the impulses and intentions that drive us. It reveals our courage and boldness in action, which may become rash and impulsive. It indicates will and ambition, the forces we project in life.

Specific Indications: Success through one's own efforts. Adventures. Younger brothers and sisters. All desires. Life, energy, excitement, enthusiasm. Initiative, motivation. Courage, bravery, fear. Voice, singing, fine arts, music, dance, drama. Musicians, actors, dancers, and singers. Managers, organizers, detailed work. Hearing, right ear. The hands, arms, shoulders. Letters, writing, journals, all communications. Firmness of personality (mental stability—but not the mind). Travel— short journeys. Matters relating to communication such as writing. Shows the acquisitive or motivated side of our nature.

Karaka planet: Mars.

Type of house: The 3rd house is a *dusthana* (suffering) house, but only very slightly, as well as an *upachaya* (increasing) house.

Although expenses are ruled by the 12th house, a person may spend constantly because of a very powerful or significant 3rd house since this is the house that rules our desires.

THE FOURTH HOUSE

The 4th House *(Shukha Bhava)* has an affinity with Cancer and the Moon.

Key Words: Emotional environment.

Relates to mother, home and emotional happiness.

The 4th house is associated with one's personal home environment. Specifically this refers to the parents, and the emotional atmosphere at home. Planets in this house will describe the kind of home one is attracted to, and the sort of activities that take place in the home.

This house is also connected to the experience of our mother. Planets here express themselves in a private and intimate manner, showing close family bonds. Difficult planetary placements will show the troubles one has in domestic matters. This house shows emotional identification and a sense of belonging.

Vedic astrology also associates this house with one's level of contentment and happiness, the heart and emotions, psychological well-being, and the ability to attract comforts and luxuries into one's life.

The 4th house shows land and property and our ability to acquire them. As the house of property generally it shows the vehicles we may possess (Conveyances—more expensive personal property.)

Specific Indications: Mother, Happiness and contentment. The heart, emotions and happiness. Fixed assets, (such as land, buildings, property, real estate, gardens, agricultural and farm land). Paternal house and property. Comforts, luxuries. Conveyances (cars, boats, planes). Formal education (school), academic education (to an extent). Endings, the close of life, the grave.

Karaka planets: Moon and Mercury.

Type of House: The 4th house is a *kendra* (angular) house.

THE FIFTH HOUSE

The 5th House *(Putra Bhava)* has an affinity to Leo and the Sun.

Key Words: Children, Creativity.

Relates to our soul nature and creative intelligence.

The 5th House is associated with our creative self-expression, and the building up of a sense of identity and security through a trust in oneself. Planets here reflect the course of self-development in childhood and the ability to play and to be joyful and spontaneous. Later in life, this is reflected in our relationship with children and whether we choose to have children of our own. Creative activity, sport, romantic enjoyment, joy, pleasures and love affairs are associated with this house. The 5th is also connected with our ability to take risks through speculation, gambling and investments. Vedic astrology also associates this house with the visual creative arts (such as painting), intelligence and *purva punya*—karmic rewards due from one's previous incarnation.

Traditionally the house of children, though for women the 5th house from the Moon is often more important for children than the 5th from the ascendant. Conception, pregnancy and childbirth are all associated with this house.

Specific Indications: Children, the mind, intelligence. *Purva punya* (rewards or credit due from last incarnation). Sense of destiny. Pleasures. Speculation, gambling, investments. Love affairs, romance, love from spouse. Kingship, government, rulers, politicians. Spiritual techniques, mantras, religious practices or rituals. Capacity to advise others. Morals, good deeds, charity, generosity. Merit, fine qualities, integrity, humility, ability. Religious tendencies. Pleasures, fun, sport. Art of painting and drawing.

Karaka planets: Jupiter.

Type of house: The 5th house is a *kona* (trinal) house.

THE SIXTH HOUSE

The 6th House *(Satru Bhava)* has an affinity with Virgo and Mercury.

Key Words: Health and service.

Relates to health and disease, work and the service of others.

The 6th House is related to the ability of the individual to integrate with their working environment. Daily jobs, menial work, routines, labor and all the necessary duties of life, are reflected in this house. Planets placed here show, amongst other things, the kind of advantages or difficulties that are experienced in our working relationships. Planets here will also indicate the kind of work one is involved in, the colleagues one relates to in the workplace, and one's level of service to others.

This house also shows the state of bodily functions—in other words it is connected with health on a physical level. An interest in medicine and healing skills, as well as nutrition, diet and food preparation are also related to this house.

Vedic astrology also associates financial worries, enemies and competitors with the 6th house.

Specific Indications: Health, illness, disease. Enemies, competitors (seen or unseen), foes, jealous people. Daily jobs, service jobs. Food and the preparation of food, restaurants, caterers. Appetite. Subordinates, such as workers tenants, maids, employees. Maternal uncle. Medical profession, nursing, doctors. Cousins. Debts. Litigation.

Karaka planets: Mars and Saturn.

Type of house: The 6th house is a *dusthana* (suffering) house, as well as an *upachaya* (increasing) house.

THE SEVENTH HOUSE

The 7th House *(Kalatra Bhava)* has an affinity with Libra and Venus.

Key Words: Marriage and long term relationship.

Indicates all important partnerships.

The 7th House is connected with social relationships—daily contact with other people on a social level. Whereas the 1st House represents the self, the 7th represents "others." Planets here show the kind of people one chooses to relate to on a consistent, long-term basis and is thus naturally related to the marriage partner.

In reality planets in the 7th house show qualities that we tend to underrate or deny in ourselves but appreciate in others, or even projects onto others, particularly our close partners. Both enemies and loved ones are indicated by this house, as both are connected with the phenomenon of projection.

Being 10th from the 10th house, one's public image and the attainment of positions or posts can be indicated by this house.

Specific Indications: The spouse, married life. All long-term relationships, partnerships. Sexual passions, desire. Residence in foreign countries. Courts. Veins and loins.

Karaka planets: Venus.

Type of house: The 7th house is a *kendra* (Angular) house, and also a *maraka* (killer) house.

THE EIGHTH HOUSE

The 8th House *(Ayur Bhava)* has an affinity to Scorpio and Mars.

Key Words: Hidden resources. Longevity.

Related to sex, death, the occult, vice, and the hidden side of life.

The 8th House is associated with our private intimate relationships with others—with unspoken emotions which tend to be suppressed during the course of the day. As such the 8th house is related to the ability to show sexual intimacy, and the strength of sexual desire. Planets placed here will show the ease or difficulty that we may experience in lowering emotional defences. There can be much emotional anxiety and trauma connected with this house. Planets placed here will be hidden in their expression and reflect unresolved emotional issues. The 8th house also reflects the emotions evoked in others.

This house is also related to the finances of others in so far as they have an impact on our own lives, such as inheritance.

Indications include other people's money, joint finances, partners wealth and alimony, as well as with financial loans, banks, and tax authorities.

Unforeseen breaks and changes to the pattern of one's life are also associated with the 8th house.

It is also related to an interest in occult and psychological powers, death and beyond death states. It can give indications regarding longevity, accidents, chronic long term illness and the nature of our experience of death.

Specific Indications: Life force, longevity. Means of death, experience of death. Wills and legacies, insurance benefits. Joint finances, partners money, monetary gains from partner, alimony. The reproductive system. Sexual strength and attractiveness, venereal diseases, sexual desires, and fantasies. Chronic and longterm illnesses of any kind. Misfortunes, accidents. Occult subjects, secretive matters. Controversy, Intuition and psychic abilities.

Karaka planet: Saturn.

Type of house: the 8th house is a *dusthana* (suffering) house.

THE NINTH HOUSE

The 9th House *(Bhagya Bhava)* has an affinity to Sagittarius and Jupiter.

Key Word: deeper understanding.

Shows our religious, philosophical or ethical principles or opinions.

The 9th House is related to the need to gain deeper insight and understanding of life. It refers to the individual's personal experience or lack of spiritual or philosophical perceptions. It is also connected with higher education, intellectual convictions, and ability to mentally or spiritually influence others.

The 9th house shows the need to expand personal horizons through education or travel.

Planets placed here will show the nature and form of the insight which dawns during the course of one's life and the attitude one has to spiritual and intellectual authorities. An emphasis on this house often indicates one who travels abroad frequently, has overseas connections or is influenced by other cultures or their religions.

Vedic astrologers frequently associates the father with this house. It shows the influences and authorities that inspire and guide us. Being the 5th from the 5th house we can sometimes gain additional information regarding our children.

This is the house of grace, fortune and luck, often bringing sudden and unexpected gains into our life. Those who win lotteries or races usually have good influences associated with this house.

Specific Indications: The father. Grandchildren. Luck, fortune, solutions to problems. Religion, philosophy, morals. Faith, worship. A person's guru, spiritual teachers, elders, travel, long journeys. Wisdom, higher knowledge of all kinds, higher education. Law. Performance of good deeds, charity, virtue.

Karaka planets: Jupiter and the Sun.

Type of house: The 9th house is a *kona* (trinal) house.

Good planets here can go very far to counteract any negative influences in the chart.

Note regarding the father: The 9th house represents the father as teacher and guide whereas the 10th house, also mentioned in some texts as being the house of the father, represents the father as an authority figure.

THE TENTH HOUSE

The 10th House *(Karma Bhava)* has an affinity with Capricorn and Saturn.

Key Word: Achievement.

Indicates our public status in life and our achievements in the material world.

The 10th House is related to concrete professional achievements in life, and to one's personal ambitions. Planets placed here will show what kind of relationship one has to people in authority and the kind of executive talent one possesses. This is a most powerful and influential house and planets placed here are capable of bestowing public prominence and professional success. Fame, honour, status and deeds performed to benefit society all fall under the domain of this house.

The 10th house does not in itself determine the career—the 1st house and other factors should also be considered important in this regard. What it *does* show is the degree of success in our chosen career or profession, the effects of our actions on the world and the status we are able to achieve in life.

Specific Indications: Career, professional activities. The Dharma or life purpose. Fame, honour, status, respectability. Worldly power. Holy pilgrimages. Good deeds, activities that benefit society. The head of an institution, authority figures, eminent persons, government officials, government work.

Karaka planets: Mercury, Sun, Jupiter, and Saturn.

Type of House: The 10th house is a *kendra* (angular) house as well as an *upachaya* (increasing) house.

As the highest point in the chart, planets here are generally very dynamic and can serve to raise us up in life.

THE ELEVENTH HOUSE

The 11th House *(Laba Bhava)* has an affinity with Aquarius and Saturn.

Key Words: Social involvement. Gains.

Refers to our aspirations and goals, as well as intelligence and friendship.

In Western astrology the 11th House is associated with friendships, groups and other kinds of social relationships and shows the need to create a secure social life. It is also related to social ideals, and planetary energy here will often be implemented socially or politically in some form of group involvement.

In Vedic astrology the emphasis on this house is more on the way that it represents our goals, ambitions and desires, the hopes and dreams we have for the future, not just for our self, but for people in general. Planets placed here will show the ease or difficulty we experience in social integration, first of all at school, and later in the social circles with which we tend to involve ourselves. The 11th house is also connected with financial gains and fluctuations due to income from sudden ventures or sideline jobs.

Whatever is placed in this house grows and increases. This is the only house where all planets, whether benefic or malefic are considered good in that they add to the person's income.

Specific Indications: Major goals, ambitions, and desires. Opportunities. Gains and profits by any means (wealth). Sudden financial fluctuations. Supplemental income, wealth from sideline jobs or sudden ventures. Gains through profession. Eldest sibling. Paternal uncle. Legs and ankles.

Karaka planet: Jupiter.

Type of house: The 11th house is an *upachaya* (increasing) house. This is the strongest upachaya house.

THE TWELFTH HOUSE

The 12th House *(Vraya Bhava)* has an affinity with Pisces and Jupiter.

Key Word: Dissolution.

Refers to our subconscious and hidden emotional nature.

The 12th House is the most subtle of all the houses and planets placed here express their energies in a most secluded and private manner. This house represents the inner world of the psyche, so planets in the 12th express themselves on a more psychic or spiritual level, feeding our inner world of dreams, fantasy and imagination. This house and planets therein represent the dissolution of worldly interests and material ambitions and the ascendancy of subconscious influences.

This house is also related to sickness and to isolated institutions such as prisons, hospitals, and monastic institutions. Traditionally it has always been associated with secret enemies, confinement, and deprivation of liberty. Vedic astrology places sexual pleasures and secret or clandestine relationships within the domain of this house, as well as, at the other extreme, after death states, Self-realization, salvation or liberation from rebirth.

Specific Indications: Loss, expenditure, expenses, debts, misfortune. Moksha, Self-realization, enlightenment, final liberation, salvation. The state after death (heaven or hell), *lokas*, or planes of existence. The bedroom, bedding. Pleasures of the bed (sexual pleasure). "Unknown places" (remote, far-off countries). Travel to foreign lands, life in remote countries. Hospitals, prisons, and other places of confinement. Hearing, the left ear. Vision, the left eye. Feet, anus. Waste. Experience with thieves and robbers. Secret enemies.

Karaka planet: Saturn.

Type of House: The 12th house is a *dusthana* (suffering) house.

If Jupiter is in the 12th house, the person becomes skilled in their work, whether domestic or business, at a comparatively young age. It also inclines one to be benevolent and charitable by nature.

THE ARRANGEMENT OF THE HOUSES

In Vedic astrology the houses are considered to be very important. Planetary placements by house are generally given as much, if not more, emphasis and attention than their sign positions. For this reason it becomes important not only to understand the meanings of the twelve houses but also to have a thorough grasp of the relationship of each house to the Ascendant.

To review, in the traditional Vedic system the whole of the rising sign corresponds to the first house, the whole of the second sign corresponds to the second house, and so on. Thus if Virgo is the sign on the Ascendant, any planets in Virgo are considered to be in the first house, any planets in Leo would be in the twelfth house, and any planets in Libra would be in the second house. This method of house division is known as the "House = Sign" method. For those who are familiar with the more complex methods of house division used in Western astrology this may seem a rather crude and primitive approach to house division, although greater familiarity with the Vedic system will reveal the value and effectiveness of this method—in short, it works!

Angular *(Kendra)* Houses

After the 1st house/Ascendant, the most vital and important houses are the 4th, 7th and 10th. Any planets in the 7th and 10th houses will have a direct impact on the Ascendant, although planets in any of these four angular houses will have a considerable influence on one's life. Planets placed in the 10th house are often the most influential planets in the whole chart.

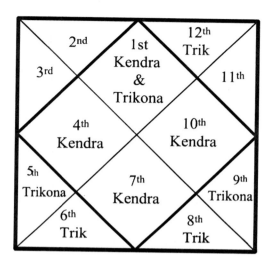

Trinal *(Trikona)* Houses

The 1st, 5th and 9th houses (known as trinal or *trikona* houses) are capable of bringing much good fortune. The nature of the 5th and 9th is gentle and auspicious. Planets located in them are capable of doing much good.

The angular houses are related to the divine masculine energy—*Vishnu,* while the trinal houses relate to the divine feminine energy—*Lakshmi.* The first house is classified as both an angular and a trinal house, and as such it blends both the masculine and the feminine energies. This is one of the reasons that the 1st house and the planet that rules it are considered so important. They are strong and balanced due to the union of the masculine and feminine polarities.

Trik or *Dusthana* Houses

The 6th, 8th, and 12th houses are considered inauspicious. They carry negative energies related to, among other things, disease (6th), death (8th) and loss (12th). In Sanskrit these three houses are referred to as *Dusthana* or *Trik* indicating that they are houses associated with sorrow or suffering.

Planets that rule these houses can cause difficult conditions to manifest, even if they are planets that are considered auspicious, such as Venus or Jupiter. The 8th and 12th houses are considered rather more difficult than the 6th in terms of their ability to cause suffering, yet they have another side to them in that they can indicate elevation to higher states of consciousness, and are often found emphasized in the chart of those who have strong spiritual or mystical aspirations. The 4th, 8th and 12th houses are known as *moksha* or "liberation" houses—areas of the chart which are associated with the elevation of consciousness.

The Third and Eleventh Houses

The 6th from the 6th house is the 11th, and the 8th from the 8th house is the 3rd house. For this reason the 3rd and 11th houses are considered somewhat inauspicious. This inauspicious quality especially applies to a planet that happens to rule both the 3rd and the 11th house signs.

Upachaya Houses

The 3rd, 6th, 10th and 11th houses are also referred to as *upachaya,* a Sanskrit term which means increasing or improving, as any planet placed in these houses tends to increase in strength and influence with the passage of time. This especially applies to the 11th house, where planets gradually strengthen and improve in quality and influence. Planets placed in the 11th are capable of improvement, although, as previously mentioned, the lord of the 11th always carries inauspicious tendencies.

The *Upachaya* houses are places of growth and expansion. Planets located in these houses will yield benefits as a result of our personal efforts. The better the planet (by sign placement and aspect) the greater the potential to render benefits. Malefic planets naturally demand more effort in order for them to yield good results, while benefics render positive results with just a little conscious effort.

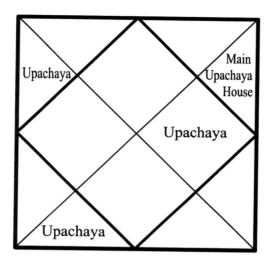

Maraka Houses

The word *maraka* is a difficult word to translate. It literally means "killer," although its real meaning in an astrological context is the propensity to cause death or to be detrimental to our health or longevity.

The *maraka* houses are the 2nd and the 7th. This is because the 7th house is 12th from the 8th (longevity). Being 12th from the 8th it represents the loss of longevity. The 2nd house is 12th from the 3rd house, which also represents longevity. Being 8th from the 8th house, the 3rd house also reflects the 8th house qualities (see next section: *Bhavat bhavam*). The term *maraka* is applied both to the 2nd and 7th houses and to the planets that rule the signs found on the 2nd and 7th houses. If the rulers of the 2nd or 7th are also placed *in* one of these houses or if the same planet owns both the 2nd and 7th houses, as happens for those with Aries or Libra Ascendants, that planet becomes very strong in maraka qualities.

Of the two *maraka* houses, the 2nd house (and the planet which rules it) are considered to posses stronger *maraka* properties than the 7th house and its ruler. You should not be unduly concerned regarding *maraka* planets – their role in determining longevity.

Length of life is modified by a variety of other factors. Remember that the ruler of the 2nd house is also capable of bestowing wealth and prosperity.

Bhavat bhavam

Bhavat bhavam is a Sanskrit phrase that means "from house to house." The best way to explain bhavat bhavam is with an example. The 7th house *(bhava)* is indicative of the spouse (or partner in general), and the 6th house is indicative of health. As such, the 6th house from the 7th house, which is the 12th, indicates the health of the spouse. Similarly, the 9th (morals) from the 7th (spouse), which is the 3rd, represents the moral character of the spouse.

Using this technique of *bhavat bhavam* we can find all the secondary and not so obvious meanings of the houses. This is important when trying to answer specific questions about a birth chart, such as "Will my children earn a good living?"

Mantreshwara says:

"Whenever the effects of any *bhava* [house] are to be determined in the case of a nativity, that *bhava* should be considered as the *lagna* [ascendant] and the effects of the 12 *bhavas* reckoned from such as 1st (form), 2nd (wealth) etc., should be examined and declared. In the same way the effects of the father, mother, brother, maternal uncle, son, husband, and servant should be determined by treating the signs occupied by their respective *Karakas*, viz., the sun, moon and other planets, in the nativity as the *lagna*." – *Phaldeepika 15:20,21*

Summary of the Houses

Angular *(kendra)* houses:
The first, fourth, seventh and tenth houses are called angular houses or kendra houses.

Trines *(trikona)* houses:
The fifth and ninth houses are called trines or trikona houses. First house is also considered as a trine.

Trik (Dusthana) houses:
The sixth, eighth and twelfth houses are called trik houses or dusthana houses.

Neutral Houses:
The second, third and eleventh houses are sometimes classified as neutral houses.

Angles and trines are auspicious houses while *dusthanas* are inauspicious. Neutral houses can make both positive and negative contributions to the overall interpretation of the chart. On occasions the "neutral" houses are capable of producing great good and in some situations can create a variety of problems and difficulties.

The Planets as *Karaka* for the Houses

Karaka planets were briefly mentioned earlier. Each of the twelve houses is represented by one or more planets. In making an assessment of the strength or weakness of a particular house it is important that you should always take into consideration the planet(s) which acts as the house *karaka* (representative) even though the planet may have no other connection with that house. For example, if you are making an assessment of the 1st house, also consider the condition of the Sun; if the house under consideration is the 5th look also at Jupiter, and so on. The following table shows these karakas:

Houses	Karaka Planet(s)
1st	Sun
2nd	Jupiter
3rd	Mars
4th	Moon and Mercury
5th	Jupiter
6th	Mars and Saturn

7th	Venus
8th	Saturn
9th	Jupiter and Sun
10th	Mercury, Sun, Jupiter & Saturn
11th	Jupiter
12th	Saturn

Both Parashara and Jaimini, two highly respected authorities on Vedic Astrology, gives only one *karaka* planet for each house. If you wish to follow their example then consider only the first mentioned planet for each house in the above tabulation.

The significance of houses fructify under the planetary periods (the *Dashas*) connected with them. The nature and extent of house significations are dependent on three important factors:

(1) The strength of the lord of the house; (2) strength of the significator *(karaka)* of the house; and (3) The effects on the house itself due to the occupation or aspects of planets. The significations of the houses suffer if their lords and significators are weak or if they or their lords are under the influence of functional malefic planets.

CHAPTER EIGHT

PLANETARY ASPECTS

"All the planets aspect the 3rd and 10th houses with quarter sight; the 5th and 9th house with half sight, the 4th and 8th houses with three-quarters sight, and the 7th house with full sight; but Saturn aspects the 3rd and 10th with full sight, Jupiter aspects the 5th and 9th with full sight, and Mars aspects the 4th and 8th with full sight." – *Brihat Jataka 2.13*

In Jyotish, an aspect cast by a planet is termed its *Drishti* (glance). *Drishti* is the ability of a planet to project its energy to other areas of the chart by influencing signs of the zodiac other than the one in which it resides. Each planet casts full strength aspects, three-quarter strength aspects, half strength aspects, and quarter strength aspects. In practice only the full strength aspects are regarded as important in birth chart delineation.

Here are the general principles of *drishti:*

- All aspects are counted from sign to sign, the count beginning from the sign occupied by the planet concerned.
- All aspects are counted in an counterclockwise direction if using the North Indian chart diagram—clockwise if using the South Indian diagram.

Full Aspects

All planets cast an aspect on the sign/house opposite to the one in which they are located. This is called the 7th house aspect. Any planets residing in this sign/house will receive the full aspect of the planet. Example: Sun in the 2nd house would be fully aspecting Mars if it were placed in the 8th house.

Mars, Jupiter and Saturn have additional full aspects.

Mars always aspects the 4th, 7th and 8th houses from the house of its location. Example: Mars in 7th house would aspect the 10th, 1st and 2nd houses, as well as any planets located in these houses.

Jupiter always aspects the 5th, 7th and 9th houses from the house in which it is located. Example: Jupiter in the 5th house would aspect the 9th, 11th and 1st houses.

Saturn always aspects the 3rd, 7th and 10th houses from the house in which it is located. Example: Saturn in the 7th house would aspect the 9th, 1st and 4th houses.

We will now look for all of the full strength aspects existing between planets in the birth chart of Margaret Thatcher.

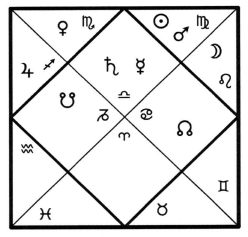

- Sun aspects the 6th house (with its 7th aspect).
- Moon aspects the 5th house (with its 7th aspect).
- Mars aspects Jupiter in the 3rd house (with its 4th aspect), the 6th house (with its 7th aspect), and the 7th house (with its 8th aspect).
- Mercury aspects the 7th house (with its 7th aspect).
- Jupiter aspects the 7th house (with its 5th aspect), the 9th house (with its 7th aspect), and the Moon in 11th house (with its 9th aspect).
- Venus aspects the 8th house (with its 7th aspect).
- Saturn aspects Jupiter in the 3rd house (with its 3rd aspect),

- the 7th house (with its 7th aspect), and Rahu in the 10th house (with its 10th aspect).

Another way of expressing full aspects, stated in degrees rather than houses follows:

- All planets cast a full aspect 180 degrees away from their position; this is called the 7th house aspect.

Mars, Jupiter, and Saturn have these additional aspects:

- Mars casts a full aspect 90 and 210 degrees ahead of its location; these are called the 4th and 8th house aspects, respectively.
- Jupiter casts a full aspect 120 and 240 degrees (known as its 5th and 9th house aspects).
- For Saturn, the additional aspects are 60 and 270 degrees ahead of its location (known as its 3rd and 10th house aspects).

This second method of expressing the aspects is more precise in that <u>the closer the aspect is to the exact degree distance the more potent it becomes</u>. For example, for a Scorpio Ascendant, if Saturn is in 12 degrees of Leo in the 10th house and the Moon is in 13 degrees of Libra in the 12th house, we say that Saturn aspects the Moon through its 3rd house aspect. Expressed in degrees, the distance between them is 61 degrees. This is only 1 degree more than the exact 60 degree aspect mentioned above, making the aspect of Saturn on the Moon a very potent one. If the Moon had been situated at 29 degrees of Libra it would still be considered fully aspected by Saturn, but not as powerfully as in the first example. In the first example the influence of Saturn on the Moon would have been full strength. However, if Saturn had been at 1 degree Leo and the Moon at 29 degrees Libra the impact of the aspect would be lessened.

When a planet aspects a sign its as if that planet throws a switch that lights up the whole of the aspected sign, including any planets that may be occupying that sign.

However, the degree area of the aspected sign that corresponds to the degree area of the planet casting the aspect will be the most illumined area of that sign.

There is controversy regarding the aspects of Rahu and Ketu. Some jyotishis do not assign any aspecting power to them, while others assign the same aspects as Jupiter (the 5th and 9th house aspects). Form your own judgement on this matter as you become more experienced in chart interpretation.

Finer Aspects

We have spoken above of full aspects. And in most cases this is quite adequate for judging the planetary influences of a birth chart. Yet if we go back to the very early texts from which jyotish originated it will be found that every planet is considered to possess all of the above-mentioned aspects to some extent. Thus it may be said that:

- Every planet aspects its opposite (7th or 180°) house 100%.
- All planets have 75% aspect strength on the houses which are 4th (90°) and 8th (210°) from them except Mars, which has 100% strength aspect on these positions.
- All planets have 50% aspect strength on the houses which are 5th (120°) and 9th (240°) from them except Jupiter, which has 100% strength aspect on these positions.
- All planets have 25% aspect strength on the houses which are 3rd (60°) and 10th (270°) from them except Saturn, which has 100% strength aspect on these positions.

As already mentioned, it is normal practice to consider only the full 100% aspects of the planets. The weaker aspects can be safely ignored unless their degree distance is exact or a very detailed analysis is being undertaken.

An aspect is determined to be harmful or beneficial depending on the planets involved. Any aspect between Mars and Saturn (both natural malefics) would be considered difficult, while if we were to consider an aspect between Moon and Jupiter (in opposition, in which the Moon and Jupiter mutually aspect each other) it would be highly beneficial.

Conjunction

Just as planets have no aspect on signs/house that are 2nd, 6th, 11th or 12th from the sign/house which they occupy, so planets sharing the same sign/house are not considered in aspect to each other. However, occupying the same sign and house creates a commingling of planetary energies. If the planets are within $10°$ degrees of each other, a definite conjunction or exchange of their energies takes place. Further apart, they still form a connection, although the impact becomes weaker as the distance increases.

Mutual aspects

Frequently aspects are only one way. For example Mars in the 10th house may fully aspect the Sun in the 1st house with its 4th aspect, but the Sun does not aspect Mars with a full aspect—the influence is only one way, with the Sun on the receiving end of the Mars influence. If two planets mutually aspect each other then there is a crossfertilization of planetary energies and the interpretation of the combination becomes a little more complex—depending on the "chemistry" of the planets concerned.

When two planets fully aspect each other they are said to have *sambhanda,* a Sanskrit word which means a shared connection or shared relationship. *Sambhanda* is a word also used to describe several other ways in which two planets are mutually connected. For example if two planets exchange signs (such as Moon in Capricorn and Saturn in Cancer), or if planet A aspects planet B and planet B occupies a sign owned by planet A, the planets concerned would be said to be in *sambhanda*, or mutually linked. Even when two planets share the same sign they have *sambhanda* with each other.

10th House Influence

Another consideration is that when a planet is in the 10th sign/ house from another it has a significant influence on it, even though it is not casting a full (100%) aspect. This seems particularly true of a planet situated in the 10th house, from which position it will influence the Ascendant/1st house and any planets therein. Again, the closer the aspect (90 degrees) between the planet in the 10th house and the Ascendant point or a occupying the 1st house the more potent the influence becomes.

Tajika Aspects

The following information on *Tajika* and *Jaimini* aspects is given for the sake of completeness.

These are very similar to the aspects used by Western astrologers. The *Tajika* aspects are the conjunction (0°), opposition (180°), square (90°), trine (120 °) and sextile (60°).

Tajika aspects were expounded in detail by Neelakantha, an Indian astrologer who lived during the 16th century. These are the very same aspects as the five major aspects (conjunction, opposition, square, trine, and sextile) used in Western astrology, which measure aspects from planet to planet rather than from planet to sign. The orbs (the allowance of deviation from an exact aspect) used by Neelakantha are the same as those recommended by William Lilly, the 17th century English astrologer.

Although these aspects are used for natal chart delineation in the West, in India they have been used mainly for *Prashna* (Horary or "question chart") astrology or for judging Annual (Solar Return) charts. If we applied them to natal chart interpretation we would be moving very close to the Western method of aspect interpretations. In "The Astrology of the Seers" the Vedic astrologer David Frawley recognizes that these aspects have some validity and that it may be helpful to take them into consideration when interpreting the Vedic natal chart.

The orbs of planets given by Neelakantha and William Lilly are:

Planet	Orb
Sun	15 degrees
Moon	12 degrees
Mercury	7 degrees
Venus	7 degrees
Mars	8 degrees
Jupiter	9 degrees
Saturn	9 degrees

In order to establish the orb between two planets, add together their individual orbs and divide by 2. Suppose you want to establish whether Venus is in trine with the Jupiter. The orb of the Jupiter is 9 degrees and that of Venus is 7 degrees. Add them together and divide by 2. The result is 8 degrees, which is the maximum distance for deviation from an exact trine (120 degree) aspect.

Jaimini Aspects

Another method of using aspects has been expounded by the sage Jaimini. According to Jaimini every cardinal (movable) sign aspects every fixed sign except the one adjacent to it. In the same way all fixed signs aspect every cardinal sign with the exception of the one adjacent to it. Mutable (common) signs aspect each other.

These aspects are not only given in the principle *Jaimini* text, the *Jaimini Sutras*, but are also found in Parashara's classic *Brihat Parashara Hora Shastra*. Even so, the description of the aspects (*drishti*) given previously in this text are the ones referred to as the *Parashari* aspects and are the most widely used method of judging aspects in a natal chart. Until you become an experienced jyotishi you should avoid trying to combine *Parashari* system of aspects with the *Tajika* or *Jaimini* systems.

CHAPTER NINE

THE ALL IMPORTANT ASCENDANT

"Whichever house is occupied by the lord of the Ascendant, the well-being of that house is assured." – *Phaldeepika 15.9*

The Ascendant Sign constitutes the first house of your birth chart. The Ascendant plays a crucial role in determining your general health and well-being, and colors the interpretation of practically every factor of your chart. The Ascendant determines not only your Ruling Planet, but the house rulership of every other planet.

Some Ascendants are better than others for giving good health and vitality. Remember that the signs are divided by polarity, quality and element. These classifications should be applied to the ascending sign in order to understand the constitution and basic orientation of the personality.

The cardinal signs are active and initiatory by nature; fixed signs manifest a centralizing energy which is resistant to change, while the mutable signs are more fluid and adaptable by nature.

The fire energy is aspirational and creative. The earth energy is stable and grounded. Air is flexible, mental and communicative. Water is sensitive, intuitive and emotional.

The three qualities repeat their sequence four times in succession and the four elements repeat their sequence three times, beginning with Aries and ending in Pisces. Thus Aries is Cardinal Fire, Taurus is Fixed Earth, Gemini is Mutable Air, Cancer is Cardinal Water and so on. The six odd numbered signs in the sequence (Aries, Gemini, Leo, Libra, Sagittarius, Aquarius) are considered to be more positive, externalizing and outgoing whereas the even numbered signs (Taurus, Cancer, Virgo, Scorpio,

Capricorn and Pisces) are considered to have deeper, more internalized and passive qualities.

In Sanskrit the cardinal (movable) signs are referred to as *chara;* the fixed signs as *sthira* and the mutable (or dual) signs as *dwara.*

Aries Ascendant

Aries is a cardinal fire sign, giving an active and aspirational nature. Aries can be impulsive and headstrong. They are enterprising. Patience and persistence are not strong points. Mars becomes the ruling planet.

An Aries ascendant is considered strong if one or both of these conditions apply: the rising degree is between 0° and 3°20'; Mars is strong by sign, occupying or aspecting the ascendant.

Taurus Ascendant

Taurus is a fixed earth sign, giving a cautious and well grounded nature. They are generally reliable and trustworthy. Taurus ascendants tends to lack spontaneity but are capable of persistence and determination. Venus becomes the ruling planet.

A Taurus ascendant is considered strong if one or more of the following conditions apply: the rising degree is between 13°20' and 16°40'; Venus is strong by sign, occupying or aspecting the ascendant.

Gemini Ascendant

Gemini is a mutable air sign, giving a communicative and adaptable nature. They are rather restless and changeable, but inquisitive and intelligent. Mercury becomes the ruling planet.

A Gemini ascendant is considered strong if one or more of the following conditions apply: the rising degree is between 26°40' and 30°; Mercury is strong by sign, occupying or aspecting the ascendant.

Cancer Ascendant

Cancer is a cardinal water sign, giving a strong but sensitive nature. Cancer enjoys family life and the company of close friends, but they are not particularly intellectual or extroverted. The Moon becomes the ruling planet.

A Cancer ascendant is considered strong if one or more of the following conditions apply: the rising degree is between 0° and 3°20'; the Moon has good paksha bala; occupies a favorable sign, or is occupying or aspecting the ascendant.

Leo Ascendant

Leo is fixed fire sign, giving a steady, warm and aspirational nature. Leos like to be admired and respected. Leos have a colorful, generous, and magnanimous personality. The Sun becomes the ruling planet.

A Leo ascendant is considered strong if one or more of the following conditions apply: the rising degree is between 13°20' and 16°40'; the Sun is strong by sign, occupying or aspecting the ascendant.

Virgo Ascendant

Virgo is a mutable earth sign, giving a practical and helpful nature. They can be exacting, precise, and sometimes critical. Mercury becomes the ruling planet.

A Virgo ascendant is considered strong if one or more of the following conditions apply: the rising degree is between 26°40' and 30°; Mercury is strong by sign, free from malefic aspects and occupying or aspecting the ascendant.

Libra Ascendant

Libra is a cardinal air sign, giving a sociable and communicative nature. Libra values peace and harmony. They are sympathetic and companionable and can give a romantic or idealistic view of life. Venus becomes the ruling planet.

A Libra ascendant is considered strong if one or more of the following conditions apply: the rising degree is between 0° and 3°20'; Venus is strong by sign, occupying or aspecting the ascendant.

Scorpio Ascendant

Scorpio is a fixed water sign, giving a determined but sensitive nature. A Scorpio ascendant is not always easy to understand due to an intense, secretive, or introverted personality. Mars becomes the ruling planet.

A Scorpio ascendant is considered strong if one or more of the following conditions apply: the rising degree is between 13°20' and 16°40'; Mars is strong by sign, occupying or aspecting the ascendant.

Sagittarius Ascendant

Sagittarius is a mutable fire sign, giving an active and aspirational nature. They like to be honest and direct with others. They usually posses an uncomplicated and likeable personality. Jupiter becomes the ruling planet.

A Sagittarius ascendant is considered strong if one or more of the following conditions apply: the rising degree is between 26°40' and 30°; Jupiter is strong by sign, occupying or aspecting the ascendant. (Note: Jupiter aspecting or occupying *any* ascendant will benefit that ascendant.)

Capricorn Ascendant

Capricorn is a cardinal earth sign, giving a practical and ambitious nature. They tend to take life seriously and can sometimes be a little too serious and cautious in their approach to life. Saturn becomes the ruling planet.

A Capricorn ascendant is considered strong if one or more of the following conditions apply: the rising degree is between 0° and 3°20'; Saturn is strong by sign, occupying or aspecting the ascendant.

Aquarius Ascendant

Aquarius is a fixed air sign, giving strong opinions and a communicative nature. They often have an inventive and original turn of mind. Aquarians are independent in behavior but may need to be more sensitive to the feelings and needs of others. Saturn becomes the ruling planet.

An Aquarius ascendant is considered strong if one or more of the following conditions apply: the rising degree is between 13°20' and 16°40'; Saturn is strong by sign, occupying or aspecting the ascendant.

Pisces Ascendant

Pisces is a mutable water sign, giving an adaptable, sensitive nature. Often they have an active imagination. Pisces is intuitive, idealistic or given to fantasizing and daydreaming. Jupiter becomes the ruling planet.

A Pisces ascendant is considered strong if one or more of the following conditions apply: the rising degree is between 26°40' and 30°; Jupiter is strong by sign, occupying or aspecting the ascendant.

"The Ascendant becomes strong and powerful only if it is aspected or occupied by its lord, Jupiter or Mercury but not by other planets."

– *Brihat Jataka 1.19*

Modifying Factors

All Ascendant qualities will be considerably modified by:

(a) the sign and house position of the planet which rules the Ascendant.
(b) the presence of any planets in the first house, particularly those close to the rising degree of the Ascendant sign.
(c) the aspect of any planets on the Ascendant or upon the planet which rules the Ascendant.

Just as there are planets that are natural benefics and natural malefics, so there are planets which rule malefic houses (particularly the difficult 6th, 8th, and 12th) and benefic houses (such as the 5th and 9th). Thus if Cancer is the Ascendant, the 6th house sign will be Sagittarius. As the 6th house is associated with sickness and debt, Jupiter, as ruler of Sagittarius/6th house, will become the planet that represent health problems or financial difficulties, despite being a natural benefic. For the same Ascendant (Cancer) Saturn becomes ruler of the 8th house (Aquarius) so that as well as being a natural malefic, Saturn also carries the potentially difficult 8th house energies.

This may seem to be an unnecessary complication, but it is an important consideration in the judgement of any horoscope. Jupiter ruling the 6th house can, under certain circumstances, cause problems with the liver, or with excessive self-indulgence. This does not prevent it acting beneficially and expressing its optimistic and buoyant nature in other areas of one's life. Saturn ruling a trinal house will give the ability to be grounded, patient and truthful, but ruling a difficult house may cause one to experience periods of depression, restriction or poverty.

Knowledge of a planet's house ownership will allow you to discover which particular qualities of that planet are likely to become manifest or more emphasized in a person's life. It helps us to appreciate the full scope and potential of each planet and prevents the adoption of an overly simplistic view of what each represents. In this way, the nature of each Ascendant determines which planets are particularly well disposed to it and which ones are likely to behave in the a more hostile manner.

If the planets are grouped according to the sign elements that they rule, then you will discover that the Sun, Moon, Mars and Jupiter rule fire and water signs while Mercury, Venus and Saturn each rule an earth and an air sign. The fire and water elements are associated with the emotions (fire with aspirational desires and water with feeling), while the earth and air elements have a closer affinity with the mind (earth is sensory and air rational). For this reason, in Vedic astrology there always tends to be a natural affinity and friendship between Sun/Moon (two poles of the same principle), and Mars and Jupiter. These contrast and are polarized or antagonistic towards the second group—Mercury, Venus and Saturn. If your Ascendant is ruled by a planet belonging to the first group of planets, it tends to be antagonistic towards planets belonging to the second group, and vice versa.

**Guidelines for Determining the Disposition of
Planets for Each Ascendant**

- The ruler of the Ascendant/1st house generally gives good results. Yet if it is a natural malefic or rules another house that is malefic in nature, its ability to give benefic results can be curtailed or limited and under certain circumstances it may even give negative results.
- The ruler of the 2nd house is generally neutral, though good for wealth. Yet because the 2nd is a *maraka* house this planet has the ability to negatively affect health and longevity.
- The ruler of the 3rd house is generally inauspicious (the 3rd house is 8th from the 8th house). It often has an egotistical or impulsive energy that can be rather disruptive. However it is usually good for brothers and sisters, which are associated with this house.
- The ruler of the 4th house expresses itself with strength. Natural malefics tend to display their better side when ruling angular signs but natural benefics can lose some of their positive qualities.
- The ruler of the 5th house is benevolent, as the 5th is a trinal house and gives positive results.
- The ruler of the 6th house, as a house of disease, injury and difficulty, generally gives negative results. The 6th lord is frequently associated with health problems.
- The ruler of the 7th house, as an angular house, follows the same rules as the 4th house.
- The ruler of the 8th, a house of obstacles, opposition and negativity, is inauspicious.

- The ruler of the 9th, the best *kona* or trinal house, is usually a very fortunate planet which gives positive results.
- The ruler of the 10th house follows the same rules as that of any angular ruler and represents the strongest of the angular houses.
- The ruler of the 11th is good for income and gains, which this house rules. However, it is malefic for the chart as a whole because it has a disruptive, impulsive or even anarchic influence and can cause diseases and injuries just as the 6th lord does. (Remember that the 11th is 6th from the 6th).
- The ruler of the 12th is generally inauspicious but more often neutral in character as it will usually rule another house that is less hidden and remote than the 12th.

We must not only combine the natural status of the planet with the two houses it rules but also consider its relationship with the ascendant. For example Saturn rules the 8th and 9th houses for Gemini ascendants, a good and a bad house. Saturn is a natural malefic but normally a friend of Mercury, which rules Gemini. Saturn's moolatrikona sign is Aquarius, which governs the 9th. Hence although it would give somewhat mixed results it would function in a manner that is predominantly helpful for someone with a Gemini ascendant. Planetary positions in each chart will modify these principles of house rulership.

- A planet having lordship of both the 8th and 3rd gives particularly bad results.
- The Sun or Moon owning the 8th do not become malefic, except for purposes of medical astrology, where they are damaged by this lordship. If the 8th lord owns a trine it becomes auspicious (i.e., Saturn owning the 8th and 9th for a Gemini ascendant). If the 8th lord also owns the 3rd, 6th or 11th house it can be most harmful.
- The effect rendered by the 2nd, 8th and 12th lords will depend upon their association. They contribute their main effects according to the other houses that they own.

- A planet owning both an angular house (1st, 4th, 7th, or 10th) and a trinal house (5th or 9th) attains a very important and positive status. When this occurs the planet is known as a *Raja Yoga Karaka*.
- Trinal lords always give beneficial results. Of the trinal houses, the 9th is the strongest.
- Natural benefics owning only the 4th, 7th, or 10th houses will fail to give benefic effects.
- Natural malefics owning only the 4th, 7th, or 10th houses will not be so malefic. This does not mean that the give benefic results, only that their negative impact is greatly lessened.
- Whether malefic or benefic, any planets owning the 3rd, 6th, or 11th houses have a strong propensity to produce negative results.

Relationship Of Planets To Each Ascendant

Based on the above consideration, we give the temporary status of each planet according to the Ascendant sign. Because the rules for determining them are complicated, and because various classical texts give slightly different rules for their determination, you will find small variations given in books, both ancient and modern. For this reason there is divergence of opinion in different Vedic astrology computer programs. If in doubt, always be guided by the fact that there are two groups of planets that are generally antagonistic towards each other—the Sun, Moon, Mars and Jupiter (lords of fire and water signs) on the one hand and Mercury, Venus and Saturn (lords of earth and air signs) on the other. The planet that rules the ascendant is generally on good terms with the other planets that belong to its own group.

When a planet is classified as neutral or mixed for an ascendant it means that it can give both good or bad results in different areas of life, *not* that it will only give neutral effects. The effects will not simply cancel each other out, but will be good for some things and bad for others.

ARIES ASCENDANT

Friends:	Sun, Moon, Mars and Jupiter.
Neutrals:	none
Enemies:	Mercury, Venus and Saturn .

TAURUS ASCENDANT

Friends:	Mercury, Venus and Saturn. (Saturn can be particularly auspicious).
Neutrals:	Sun.
Enemies:	Moon, Mars and Jupiter.

GEMINI ASCENDANT

Friends:	Mercury, Venus and Saturn.
Neutrals:	Moon.
Enemies:	Sun, Mars and Jupiter. (Mars can be particularly difficult).

CANCER ASCENDANT

Friends:	Moon, Mars and Jupiter. (Mars can be particularly auspicious).
Neutrals:	Sun.
Enemies:	Mercury, Venus and Saturn. (Saturn can be particularly difficult).

LEO ASCENDANT

Friends:	Sun, Mars and Jupiter. (Mars can be particularly auspicious).
Neutrals:	Moon.
Enemies:	Mercury, Venus and Saturn. (Saturn can be particularly difficult).

VIRGO ASCENDANT

Friends:	Mercury and Venus.
Neutrals:	Sun and Saturn.
Enemies:	Moon, Mars and Jupiter. (Mars can be particularly difficult).

LIBRA ASCENDANT

Friends:	Mercury, Venus and Saturn. (Saturn can be particularly auspicious).
Neutrals:	Moon.
Enemies:	Sun, Mars and Jupiter.

SCORPIO ASCENDANT

Friends:	Sun, Moon, Mars and Jupiter. (The Moon is particularly auspicious).
Neutrals:	none.
Enemies:	Mercury, Venus and Saturn.

SAGITTARIUS ASCENDANT

Friends:	Sun, Mars and Jupiter.
Neutrals:	Moon.
Enemies:	Mercury, Venus and Saturn.

CAPRICORN ASCENDANT

Friends:	Mercury, Venus and Saturn. (Venus is particularly auspicious).
Neutrals:	Moon.
Enemies:	Sun, Mars and Jupiter.

AQUARIUS ASCENDANT

Friends:	Mercury, Venus and Saturn. (Venus is particularly auspicious).
Neutrals:	none.
Enemies:	Sun, Moon, Mars and Jupiter.

PISCES ASCENDANT

Friends:	Moon, Mars and Jupiter. (The Moon is particularly auspicious).
Neutrals:	Sun.
Enemies:	Mercury, Venus and Saturn.

Friendly Planets By Sign

Enemy Planets By Sign

CHAPTER TEN

PLANETARY YOGAS

Introduction To The Study of Yogas

A unique characteristic of Vedic astrology are its *yogas*. In jyotish a yoga means a combination. Usually this is a particular combination of two or more planets. It can also mean a combination of a planet and sign or a planet and house, often involving the aspect of another planet. Sometimes more than two planets are involved. If one were to list all the various yogas given in the classical texts the number would run into thousands.

The beginner should start by understanding a few of the principle yogas that are frequently found in charts and not worry about trying to memorize a vast number of rare and rather obscure yogas. In this chapter we will be looking at some of the most important ones that are frequently encountered in birth charts.

Studying a horoscope for the presence of yogas will give you many new insights into its structure and allow you to give a deeper and more meaningful interpretation. It helps develop the intuitive and analytical abilities of the astrologer.

Every horoscope will contain yogas. Some are considered inauspicious (*ashubha* or *avayoga* yogas). Of these *dairidra* yogas will indicate poverty and *balarishta* yogas will indicate an early death. Of the beneficial yogas (*shubha* yogas) *raja* yogas indicate fame and leadership, *dhana* yogas indicate wealth and *pararava* yogas indicate renunciation of the world.

Dharma Karma Adhipati Yogas

This raja yoga, or royal yoga, which means "the combination of the lord(s) of fortune (trinal houses) and action (angular houses)." If the lord of the 5th or 9th conjoins, aspects or has *sambhanda* with the lord of the 1st, 4th, 7th or 10th this raja yoga is formed. It gives wealth, success and prominence in one's field of activity.

For some ascendants, a single planet will become lord of both an angular and a trinal house. This applies to Taurus, Cancer, Leo, Libra, Capricorn and Aquarius ascendants. For example, if one has a Taurus ascendant, Saturn rules the 9th and 10th houses. When this happens the planet becomes known as a *Raja Yoga Karaka,* and is capable of giving very desirable results.

The *Pancha Mahapurusha* Yogas

One of the most famous groups of yogas are the *Pancha Mahapurusha* yogas. *Pancha* means five and *Mahapurusha* means great person, so these are five yogas that bring greatness or distinction into a person's life.

These yogas involve one or more of the following five planets: Mars, Mercury, Jupiter, Venus or Saturn. For a *Pancha Mahapurusha* yoga to occur, the planet has to be in its own or exaltation sign as well as in an angular or trinal house. When this occurs the planet is able to express its essential nature without obstruction.

When Mars creates this yoga, known as *Ruchaka Yoga*, it makes one fearless and bold—able to confront the difficulties of life without fear. In conflicts one becomes the victor. It usually gives one abundant energy.

When Mercury creates this yoga it is known as *Bhadra Yoga*. When this occurs one is said to be learned and intelligent.

When Jupiter creates this yoga, known as *Hansa Yoga*, it makes one fortunate in life, and religious and spiritually inclined.

When Venus creates this yoga it is known as *Malavya Yoga*. This is said to make one wealthy, self indulgent and fond of the luxuries of life. It makes one fortunate in love and marriage.

When Saturn creates this yoga, known as *Shasha Yoga*, it makes one strong and disciplined. One attains positions of authority.

Pancha Mahapurusha yogas are found quite frequently in birth charts but, like many yogas, do not always seem to live up to their promise. This is not because the attributes of the yogas are faulty. Rather it is due to the budding jyotishi failing to make a correct assessment of the yoga's strengths and weaknesses. Here are some guide lines that should be applied to correctly assess the vitality and validity of these and other yogas:

- Whenever applicable, judge the yoga from both the Ascendant and the Moon Ascendant (Chandra). Using the Moon as an alternative ascendant is an important consideration in judging the strength of a yoga. For example if a *Pancha Mahapurusha* occurs both in relation to the Lagna (ascendant) and the Moon Lagna it will become much more influential.
- Consider nature of aspects on the planet(s) involved. For example, someone with *Bhadra Yoga* may not be so intelligent if Mercury is fully aspected by Saturn, or perhaps Saturn would cause their thoughts to be more serious, pessimistic or introverted.
- Consider the houses they rule. For example *Hansa Yoga* will not be so auspicious if Jupiter owns a difficult house such as the 6th or 8th.

The chart of Adolf Hitler

In this chart we have *Ruchaka* Yoga (Mars in Aries) occurring 7th from ascendant and 5th from the Moon ascendant. Combined with an exalted Sun, this makes a very powerful *Ruchaka* Yoga. Hitler was fearless, and bold - a powerful and victorious leader.

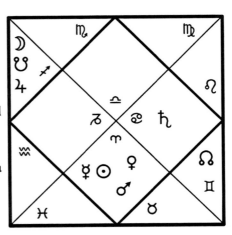

The yoga is spoiled by a potent and close aspect from Saturn in the 10th house. There is no doubt that Saturn was responsible for elevating him to political power (it becomes a *Raja Yoga Karaka* due to lordship of an angular and a trinal house), but this same planet brought out the aggressive and violent qualities of Mars which lead to his eventual defeat.

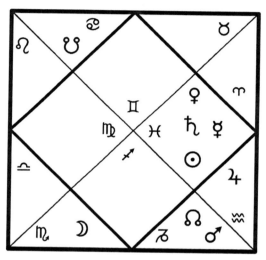

Referring back to the chart of Albert Einstein (above), we can find another example of *Pancha Mahapurusha* Yoga. In this we find *Malavya* Yoga occurring from both the Ascendant and Moon. Yet the conventional interpretation of *Malavya* Yoga would seem misleading. Only when we take into account that Venus rules the 5th house (intelligence) and also occupied the 5th from the Moon do we begin to understand that the qualities of Venus are infused with intelligence and intuitive insight. Occupying the 10th house, Venus is also joined by the lord of the 9th (higher knowledge) and the lord of the 1st, Mercury. There is a *sambhanda* (mutual exchange) between the lords of the 9th and 10th, which also helps expand our understanding of the manner in which this particular *Malavya* Yoga functions. In a similar way, we should examine every yoga found in a birth chart rather than take its conventional interpretation at face value.

One may argue that Einstein's ruling planet, Mercury, is in the sign of its fall, not what you would expect in the chart of a genius. But in Vedic astrology if a planet in its fall is associated with the presence of a planet in exaltation, the fallen state of the planet is cancelled out and is capable of behaving as if it were itself exalted. In this case the fallen planet, Mercury, is with exalted Venus and eventually behaved just as though it where in its exaltation sign. When such a reversal occurs it is technically known as *neecha bhanga* or cancellation of debility.

When interpreting *Pancha Mahapurusha* Yogas it should be born in mind that an exalted planet that occupies an angular or trinal house will give the full effects of the yoga *only* if the dispositor is strong (the dispositor is the planet which rules the sign occupied by the planet). Think of the dispositor as representing the soul or inner energy of the planet concerned.

When a planet occupies its own sign, it acts as its own dispositor and is considered strong in both body and soul. Thus a planet in its own sign can, in some circumstances, give better results than one that is exalted.

Gaja Keshari Yoga

"If Jupiter is in an angle from the Ascendant or Moon, and in conjunction with and aspected by a benefic and Jupiter is not debilitated or combust, the yoga is called Gaja Keshari." – *Brihat Parasara Hora Shastra 38.3*

For *Gaja Keshari* to occur Jupiter must be in an angle (kendra) to the Moon (1st, 4th, 7th or 10th house relationship). In this yoga, the Moon and Jupiter influence each other, giving rise to favorable results. It is said to give all round benefits such as good fortune, intelligence, a noble and virtuous nature, happiness and good education.

In judging this yoga, attention should be given to the strength *(paksha bala)* of the Moon, the signs occupied by both planets, the houses they occupy and own, aspects from other planets and so on. It would be a great mistake to declare the very auspicious results of this frequently occurring yoga without a careful analysis of all the factors involved.

Take another look at Hitler's chart. There is *Gaja Keshari* Yoga occurring in the 3rd house. This also occurs in Jupiter's own astrological sign, with the Moon owning the powerful 10th house. Thus *Gaja Keshari* becomes a powerful influence. Hitler had his share of good luck, but his intelligence and "noble virtues" became perverted and twisted. Look again and you will start to see the defects of this yoga. It occurs in the Rahu-Ketu axis of the chart (3rd – 9th) and Jupiter owns two difficult houses—the 6th and 3rd. The combination of Jupiter, Moon and Ketu in the 3rd gave rise to egotistical and grandiose desires, perverting the natural manifestation of *Gaja Keshari* Yoga.

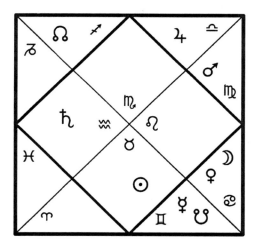

Horoscope of a Tibetan Lama (living in exile)

Another example of a powerful *Gaja Keshari* Yoga is found in the above birth chart. Here it is much more auspicious in that Jupiter owns the 5th house and the Moon is in her own sign in the 9th. The main defect is that Jupiter is in the 12th (exile) and the Moon is associated with the 12th lord (Venus). This Yoga has great spiritual potency.

Shataka Yoga

If the Moon is in the 6th, 8th or 12th house from Jupiter this yoga is formed and causes one to undergo alternating cycles of prosperity and adversity. If the Moon is in an angle to the Ascendant, this yoga is not formed.

Kemadruma Yoga

This yoga is created if there are no planets (excluding the Sun and the Nodes) in the house on either side of the Moon. The result is that the person will feel lonely and lead a poor or difficult life. Should the Moon be in either an angular or trinal house, or be in conjunction with another planet, this unfavorable yoga will be considerably neutralized. If Jupiter is angular to the Moon (*Gaja Keshari* Yoga) the yoga is cancelled out.

Sunapha Yoga

This yoga occurs when one or more planets (other than the Sun) occupy the 2nd house from the Moon. The result is that there is a greater probability of an increase in one's wealth, comfort, happiness and good reputation, particularly if the planet(s) are natural benefics. Malefics here are not so good but would not necessarily spoil the results.

Anapha Yoga

This yoga occurs when one or more planets (other than the Sun) occupy the 12th house from the Moon. The results are the same as for *Sunapha* Yoga.

Durudhara Yoga

If there are planets other than Sun occupying both the 2nd and 12th house from the Moon, this creates *Durudhara* Yoga. The results are that one earns recognition through speech, learning and a virtuous nature. It also confers wealth and a comfortable life. This is a more significant yoga than the *Sunapha* or *Anapha* yogas, although it should be emphasized that when natural benefics are involved in *Durudhara* Yoga it will give much better results. If only natural malefics (Mars and Saturn) are involved, they will do much to spoil this yoga, as would a close association of the Nodes or the Sun.

Shubha Kartari Yoga

If benefic planets occupy the 2nd and 12th houses from the Ascendant this indicates good health and the ability to accumulate wealth.

Papa Kartari Yoga

If malefic planets (not including the Nodes) occupy the 2nd and 12th houses from the Ascendant, it reverses *Shubha Kartari* Yoga, indicating poor health and financial difficulties.

Ati Vasuman Yoga

This yoga occurs if all three benefics (Mercury, Venus ad Jupiter) are in upachaya houses (3rd, 6th, 10th and 11th) from the Ascendant. It bestows abundance and prosperity.

Amala Yoga

This occurs when a natural benefic is occupying the 10th house as calculated from the Ascendant and/or the Moon (Chandra lagna). The result of this yoga is that the person develops a kind and benevolent attitude towards others. The career is likely to involve helping, caring for or serving the public in some way. One is well thought of and is likely to prosper. *Amala* means pure or spotless.

If a malefic occupies the same position the person will not be so philanthropic, although such a planet may be helpful in rather more selfish ways, perhaps causing one to maintain recognition or social standing at the expense of others.

Parivartana Yoga

This is a particular sambhanda between two planets, known in western astrology as "mutual reception." *Parivartana* yoga is said to occur when planet A is in the sign of planet B, and planet B is in the sign of planet A.

For example, if Jupiter is in Taurus and Venus is in Sagittarius, there is an exchange of signs. Jupiter is in the sign of Venus and Venus is in the sign of Jupiter. The result is that both planets will have an effect on each other similar to being in aspect or conjunction with each other. How favorable this is will naturally depend on the nature of the two planets.

Srik Yoga

This yoga occurs when only natural benefics are placed in the angular (kendra) houses. The result is that one experiences abundance, good fortune and a comfortable life.

Sarpa Yoga

With this yoga we have the reverse of *Srik* Yoga in that only natural malefics are found in the angular houses. The result is a difficult and troublesome life.

Maha Bhagya Yoga

For a man: birth occurs during the daytime and the Ascendant, Sun and Moon are placed in uneven (fire and air) signs. This is considered very fortunate as all the factors are masculine.

For a woman: birth occurs at night and the Ascendant, Sun and Moon are placed in even (earth and water) signs. Considered very fortunate for women as all the factors are feminine.

Kala Sarpa Yoga

There are very few yogas involving Rahu and Ketu. By far the most important one is *Kala Sarpa* Yoga, which occurs when all seven planets are located on one side of the axis created by Rahu and Ketu. *Kala* can mean time or black and *sarpa* means serpent. The "dark time serpent" probably refers to Ketu. The results of this yoga are said to give difficulty and hardship.

There are two types of *Kala Sarpa*; *Anuloma*, in which all the planets are moving towards Rahu, and *Viloma,* in which all the planets are moving towards Ketu. Whichever way round, one of the transiting retrograde Nodes will encounter each of the planets, creating a potential problem or crisis as it does so. There is frequently a strong energization of one's psychic nature.

With *Anuloma* Rahu's influence casts itself on all the other planets within the chart. Rahu represent illusion, ambition and worldly desire—the forces of *maya*. This form of *Kalasarpa* Yoga projects a strong current of psychic energy that can cause disruption or difficulty, particularly in the functioning of the astral body.

With *Viloma* Ketu's influence is cast over the planets, giving either spiritual aspirations and an urge towards liberation from bondage or a fixation on the past. Sometimes it gives a need to assert oneself by dominating others.

Kala Sarpa can act as an obstruction to other more positive yogas, causing obstacles, conflict or misunderstanding. It is important to consider the two houses that are involved. With *Anuloma* the house that Rahu occupies becomes an important consideration—matters related to that house are likely to be disturbed and disrupted. With the *Viloma* version of this yoga, Ketu's house becomes a key factor, full of contradictions or associated with the focus of one's spiritual interests.

Any planets in close association with the Nodes will have a significant influence. Malefics will cause the Yoga to be particularly difficult while benefics will improve it. It is also important to note the placement of the planets that rule the signs containing Rahu and Ketu. If both are well placed then this yoga can be very good. This yoga also improved if the Nodes are in compatible signs, such as Virgo-Pisces or Taurus-Scorpio.

Conclusion

These are just a small selection of yogas that are likely to be encountered when practicing astrology on a fairly regular basis. To list more would result in an overload of information.

In regard to yogas in general, avoid giving unmodified astrological interpretations of yogas found in other people's birth charts without first making a careful and integrated study of the whole horoscope.

One very frequent reason for yogas failing to materialize their promised results is that the planetary periods (dashas) of the planets involved do not occur in the appropriate periods of the person's life. Some yogas will be found to occur not only from the Ascendant but also from the Moon lagna and Sun lagna or in the *Navamsha* chart. When this happens you can be sure that the yoga will manifest its results with great strength.

A highly recommended book which gives an in-depth approach to the study of yogas is *Yogas in Astrology* by Dr. K.S. Charak. A helpful reference book to have on hand when studying yogas is *Three Hundred Important Combinations* by B.V. Raman.

CHAPTER ELEVEN

DIVISIONAL CHARTS

"If there is a preponderance of strength of benefic planets in the Shadvargas, the native will be wealthy and live a long life."

– Phaldeepika 3:11

We now come to a most interesting aspect of Vedic astrology— the Harmonic or Divisional charts. Just as we have divided the zodiac into 12 equal segments known as *rashis* or signs beginning at 0° Aries, so Vedic astrology divides each 30° rashi into smaller segments such as 15°, 12°, 10°, 3°20', and so on. Including the rashi chart, there are 16 different division charts that can be used. Each chart allows the astrologer to fine tune the indications of the rashi chart.

The Rashi chart is regarded as the primary division chart. It represents the foundation upon which the individual's life is built, and determines the principle areas of life and environment in which the planets operate. It is most important in understanding the strengths and weaknesses of the physical body, and for this reason the ancient masters of jyotish credit the Rashi chart in determining body and physique. Of course, it is more than just that, as all aspects of life are determined from it. However, the other divisional charts increase or diminish the indications and potentials shown in the main Rashi chart.

It is important to remember that none of the division charts can give information that contradicts the main Rashi chart. They can however give new insights and understanding that, once you have become familiar with them, will be found indispensable for giving a detailed and accurate astrological reading.

The most widely used of the division charts are the *Hora, Drekkana,*

Navamsha, Dwadamsha, and *Trimsamsa.* Of these five, the most important is undoubtedly the <u>Navamsha</u> chart, which in a Vedic horoscope, is nearly always shown alongside the main Rashi chart. Including the *Rashi* chart, these are referred to as the *Shadvargas* (*shad,* six and *varga,* division) or six divisional charts. Those included in this chapter are the ones most widely used.

HORA (2nd Harmonic)

"Jupiter, the Sun, and Mars give effects in the Hora of the Sun, the Moon, Venus and Saturn in the Hora of the Moon, and Mercury in the Hora of both."
– *Brihat Parasara Hora Shastra 8.13*

The *Hora* chart divides each sign in half, one half being solar and the second half lunar. *Hora* means hour. As each sign takes approximately two hours to cross over the horizon, 15 degrees or one half of a sign would only take one hour or *hora*—hence the name.

The first half of all fire and air signs (Aries, Gemini, Leo, Libra, Sagittarius and Aquarius) are solar, the second half being lunar. With the earth and water signs (Taurus, Cancer, Virgo, Scorpio, Capricorn and Pisces) it is the other way around, with the first half of the sign being lunar and the second half solar. What the *Hora* chart does is create a simple twofold zodiac representing the solar/lunar balance in the chart.

Planets that do well in the solar half of a sign are the fiery masculine planets such as the Sun, Mars and Jupiter. The cooler or more feminine planets such as the Moon, Venus and Saturn are more suited to the lunar section. Mercury, in keeping with its adaptable nature, seems happy to be in either division.

If someone has a great many planets in the solar half of the *Hora* chart that person's nature will be more active, assertive and self-confident. Someone who has a larger number of planets in the lunar half will be gentle, sensitive, intuitive and caring. Having all planets in the solar half would make someone very independent and assertive, while all planets in the lunar half would strongly indicate someone who is introverted, lacking initiative or overdependent on others.

The *Hora* chart also has a connection to the 2nd house of the Rashi chart, and for this reason is said to be related to wealth. Someone with the 2nd house lord of the Rashi chart placed in its appropriate *Hora* will find that the 2nd house indications tend to give better results.

DREKKANA (3rd Harmonic)

Each $1/3^{rd}$ division measures $10°$ (Average duration rising 40 minutes). The *Drekkana* chart divides each sign into 3 sections, each of 10 degrees. The first 10 degrees of each sign are of the same sign; the next 10 degrees ($10°$ to $20°$) belong to the next sign that is of the same element, and the final 10 degrees ($20°$ to $30°$) belongs to the third sign belonging to the same element. Thus the *Drekkanas* of Aries are Aries ($0°$ to $10°$), Leo ($10°$ to $20°$) and Sagittarius ($20°$ to $30°$). The same principle applies to each sign. Thus:

Drekkana Table

Rashi	00° to 10°	10° to 20°	20° to 30°
Aries	Aries	Leo	Sagittarius
Taurus	Taurus	Virgo	Capricorn
Gemini	Gemini	Libra	Aquarius
Cancer	Cancer	Scorpio	Pisces
Leo	Leo	Sagittarius	Aries
Virgo	Virgo	Capricorn	Taurus
Libra	Libra	Aquarius	Gemini
Scorpio	Scorpio	Pisces	Cancer
Sagittarius	Sagittarius	Aries	Leo
Capricorn	Capricorn	Taurus	Virgo
Aquarius	Aquarius	Libra	Gemini
Pisces	Pisces	Cancer	Scorpio

The *Drekkana* chart has affinities the third house in that it relates to brothers and sisters. It also indicates our courage, energy, motivation and the ability to achieve our goals and ambitions, particularly those that require enterprise and initiative. It also indicates vitality, disease and longevity (as 3rd house is 8th from 8th).

It is particularly useful for fine tuning the Ascendant, Sun and Moon (similar to the way that Western Astrology uses the Decanates).

NAVAMSHA (9th Harmonic)

Each 1/9th division measures 3°20' (Average duration rising:14 minutes). An understanding of the *Navamsha* chart is very important for anyone who is serious about the study of Jyotish. The Rashi chart has been compared to a tree and the *Navamsha* chart compared to the fruit of the tree. A tree may be tall and impressive but the fruit that it produces may taste unpleasant or sour. Another tree may look small and scrawny but produce very sweet fruits. In the same way the Rashi chart may seem very promising, but if the *Navamsha* is not supportive of the promise shown by the Rashi chart, the results will be disappointing. On the other hand, a rather ordinary looking Rashi chart may give excellent results if it is accompanied by a promising *Navamsha* chart.

Traditionally, the *Navamsha* chart is used to judge marital relationships. In this it has an affinity with the 7th house. It also has a strong connection to 9th house affairs (but not to the father), giving important indications of our spiritual purpose and future direction in life. It is also very useful in understanding the underlying strength or weakness of planets in the Rashi chart, reinforcing or undermining the potentials of the birth chart. For example, if Mars is in Aries in the Rashi chart but is placed in Cancer in the *Navamsha* chart, much of the promised strength and vitality indicated by Mars occupying its own sign is undermined. On the other hand the Moon in Scorpio in the Rashi chart but occupying Cancer in the *Navamsha* would to some extent improve the quality of the Moon, despite it being in the sign of its fall.

Vargottama *Planets*

Sometimes you will find that a planet falls in the same sign in both the Rashi and the *Navamsha* charts. When this happens the planet is classified as *vargottama*, the result being that the strength and potency of the planet is increased – for good or ill. If the planet is a benefic occupying its own sign in both the Rashi and *Navamsha*, then much good will be produced by such a planet. If a malefic planet is *vargottama* in an unfriendly sign then such a planet is capable of causing much harm.

The Nakshatras

There is an intimate connection between the 3° 20′ divisions of the *Navamsha* chart and the 27 Lunar *Nakshatras*, which constitutes a Lunar Zodiac of 27 equal divisions, each measuring 13° 20′. This Lunar Zodiac is mentioned in the Vedas and is very ancient in origin.

Each *Nakshatra* is divided into four *padas* or quarters, each of 3°20′ - each one corresponding to one of the 108 *Navamsha* divisions.

The following table shows how the signs of the zodiac are each divided into nine *navamshas (nava* means nine and *amsha* means division or section). There are a total of 108 *navamshas* (9 x 12 signs = 108) which follow the same sequence as the signs.

Navamsha Table

Rashi Sign	0.00 -3.20	3.20 -6.40	6.40 -10.00	10.00-13.20	13.20-16.40	16.40-20.00	20.00-23.20	23.20-26.40	26.40-30.00
1	1	2	3	4	5	6	7	8	9
2	10	11	12	1	2	3	4	5	6
3	7	8	9	10	11	12	1	2	3
4	4	5	6	7	8	9	10	11	12
5	1	2	3	4	5	6	7	8	9
6	10	11	12	1	2	3	4	5	6
7	7	8	9	10	11	12	1	2	3
8	4	5	6	7	8	9	10	11	12
9	1	2	3	4	5	6	7	8	9
10	10	11	12	1	2	3	4	5	6
11	7	8	9	10	11	12	1	2	3
12	4	5	6	7	8	9	10	11	12

In the above table we have replaced the sign name with its corresponding number: thus 1 stands for Aries, 2 for Taurus, 3 for Gemini and so on.

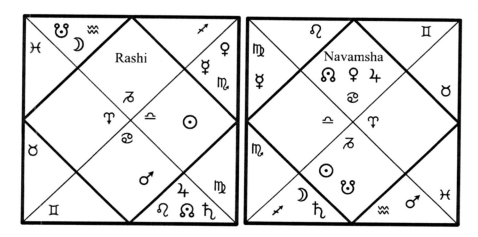

Example of a horoscope showing the Rashi and Navamsha Charts

In the Rashi chart we find that Jupiter is in Leo (the sign of a friend). In the *Navamsha* chart it is exalted in Cancer, which improves its benevolent influence and to some extent counteracts its negative placement in the 8th house with Rahu and Saturn. The Sun is in its fall in the Rashi chart. In the *Navamsha* chart it is further harmed by association with Ketu and by being in the sign of an enemy (Saturn). The Sun also becomes very influential as it occupies a kendra house in both charts.

This person lost her father, who died in tragic circumstances. This loss has deeply affected her life. In the Rashi chart, note the full aspects of Mars and Saturn on the Sun, the karaka for father, which occupies the 9th house from the Moon. This is reinforced in the *Navamsha* chart by the same two malefics hemming in the Sun by occupying the houses either side of it (in the difficult 6th and 8th houses). The Sun is also conjoined with Ketu in the *Navamsha* chart. Thus even though the *Navamsha* is not specifically used for judging the father, in this case it has reinforced our understanding of the condition of the Sun – karaka for father.

Dwadamsha Chart

Rasi	0-2.30	2.30-5	5-7.30	7.30-10	10-12.30	12.30-15	15-17.30	17.30-20	20-22.30	22.30-25	25-27.30	27.30-30
1	1	2	3	4	5	6	7	8	9	10	11	12
2	2	3	4	5	6	7	8	9	10	11	12	1
3	3	4	5	6	7	8	9	10	11	12	1	2
4	4	5	6	7	8	9	10	11	12	1	2	3
5	5	6	7	8	9	10	11	12	1	2	3	4
6	6	7	8	9	10	11	12	1	2	3	4	5
7	7	8	9	10	11	12	1	2	3	4	5	6
8	8	9	10	11	12	1	2	3	4	5	6	7
9	9	10	11	12	1	2	3	4	5	6	7	8
10	10	11	12	1	2	3	4	5	6	7	8	9
11	11	12	1	2	3	4	5	6	7	8	9	10
12	12	1	2	3	4	5	6	7	8	9	10	11

In the above table we have replaced the sign name with its corresponding number: thus 1 stands for Aries, 2 for Taurus, 3 for Gemini and so on.

DWADAMSHA (12th Harmonic)

Each 1/12th division measures 2°30'. (Average duration rising:10 minutes.) Through the dwadamsha further indications regarding one's parents can be discovered from this chart.

The *Dwadamsha* chart (or *Dwad,* as it is sometimes referred to) is used to establish information about one's parentage and ancestry (hereditary traits). It is also used to gain greater insight into one's past karma and can be used along with the Rashi chart to gain insight into past-life conditions and influences being brought forward into the present life. It relates to the subconscious mind and to hidden needs and desires that motivate us. In this connection it has a close relationship with the 12th house of the Rashi chart.

Some Jyotishis use the *Dwadamsha* chart to understand past-life influences, the Rashi for the present life situation and the *Navamsha* in order to gain greater insight into one's future and spiritual direction in life. If using it in this way, look at the placement of Saturn and the Moon in this chart—also the placement of the 12th lord of the Rashi chart.

TRIMSAMSA (30th Harmonic)

Each division is of either 5 or 8 degrees. Approximate duration rising: 20 to 30 minutes.

Trimsamsa Chart

Odd signs	0 – 5 Aries	5 – 10 Aquarius	10 – 18 Sagittarius	18 – 25 Gemini	25 – 30 Libra
Even signs	0 – 5 Taurus	5 – 12 Virgo	12 – 20 Pisces	20 – 25 Capricorn	25 – 30 Scorpio

The *Trimsamsa* is rather different from the other divisional charts. For a start it seems to have little to do with the division of a sign by 30. It consists of 5 unequal divisions and lacks any reference to Cancer or Leo. This is an important division chart for understanding major health issues or periods of misfortune.

This chart gives information regarding misfortune, disease and injuries. It has an affinity with the 6th house although a study of the 3rd, 8th, 11th and 12th houses (all related to health) should also be made. A study of the lords of these houses as well as planets placed in them, can be made in order to better determine the outcome of any indications of major difficulties, health issues or potential injuries. Traditionally, this chart is also used in female horoscopy—supposed to indicate character and faithfulness of one's wife, although not so much used in this context by present day Vedic astrologers.

The 16 Divisional Charts According To Sage Parashara

Rasi (1st Harmonic)	Fundamental chart for basic indications.
Hora (2nd Harmonic)	Wealth, Masculine/Feminine Tendencies.
Drekkana (3rd Harmonic)	Siblings, Vitality. Initiative.
Chaturthamsa (4th Harmonic)	Well-being, Happiness, Emotion.
Saptamamsa (7th Harmonic)	Children, Creative energy.
Navamsha (9th Harmonic)	Spouse, Partnerships.
Dasamsa (10th Harmonic)	Power, Position, Livelihood, Achievements.
Dwadasamsa (12th Harmonic)	Pastlife karma, Parents, Heredity.
Shodasamsa (16th Harmonic)	Property, Conveyances, Home.
Vimsamsa (20th Harmonic)	Spiritual Progress, Capacity for devotion, Religion.
Siddhamsa (24th Harmonic)	Higher education, Spiritual knowledge.
Bhamsa (27th Harmonic)	General strengths and weaknesses.
Trimsamsa (30th Harmonic)	Dangers, Misfortune, Health problems, Enmity.
Chatvarimsamsa (40th Harmonic)	Auspicious/Inauspicious effects, Good/Bad habits.
Akshavedamsa (45th Harmonic)	General indications, Moral and ethical nature.
Shashtiamsa (60th harmonic)	For fine-tuning of all planetary influences.

Guidelines for interpreting *Varga* charts

It should be remembered that unless you have a very precise birth time, the finer the harmonic division *(varga)*, the less reliable the resulting chart. Although the ascendant of the Rashi chart will change *approximately* every two hours, the *Drekkana* ascendant will change every 40 minutes.

The *Navamsha* ascendant changes every 13 minutes and 20 seconds, and the *Dwadamsha* ascendant changes every 10 minutes.

Although not listed above, for the *Nadiamsha*, which is the finest division of the zodiac used in Vedic astrology (150th of a sign), the ascendant will, on average, change every 48 seconds.

Most of the *varga* charts can be examined in the same way as the main Rashi chart, although doing this can be very confusing for the beginner. We suggest that you first apply the following guidelines to the *Navamsha* chart, and gradually introduce other *vargas* as you gain in confidence. The *varga* charts can only increase or decrease the potential shown in the Rashi chart—*they cannot contradict it.*

While some astrologers analyze *varga* charts in the same manner as the Rashi chart (judging them by taking into account house lordships, aspects and yogas), others ignore these and simply base their judgement of the *varga* chart on the strength of planetary placements by sign and the relation of planets to the lagna. Some jyotishis ridicule the employment of aspects in the division charts, questioning how aspects can occur unless one is using the Rashi chart (the 12 sign zodiac) as the only frame of reference. This assumes that astrologers know exactly what planetary aspects (drishti) are, and possibly shows a limited understanding of how they function. Our personal experience in working with divisional charts would suggest that taking account of planetary aspects yields valid insights and gives helpful information regarding our understanding of them.

The matters covered by a particular *varga* (divisional chart) will always relate to one or more houses of the Rashi chart. Examine the corresponding house that the *varga* chart represents. Be sure to take the appropriate house lord of the Rashi chart and consider its position in the *varga* chart.

Will its placement in the *varga* chart improve or damage the way that it functions in the Rashi chart? If using the *Navamsha* chart, the 7th house will be important for long term relationships and marriage while the 9th house should be studied for one's sense of purpose, fulfillment and the deeper aspects (future or spiritual indications). For example, if you wish to gain further insight into a marriage or partnership find the *Navamsha* position of the 7th lord of the Rashi chart. Does its placement in the *Navamsha* chart enhance or detract from what is indicated in the Rashi? Do the same with the appropriate karaka planet. In the above example, if we were looking at someone's relationship with their wife we would take Venus as the karaka planet. If we were looking at the husband we would examine Jupiter in the *Navamsha*.

Examine the *varga* chart for its strengths and weaknesses in terms of planets being in exaltation, own sign and fall, and placement of planets in friendly, neutral or enemy signs. This is a particularly important practice when comparing the comparative strengths of the Rashi and *Navamsha* charts.

Examine the strength of the lagna (Ascendant) of the *varga* chart and of the planet which rules the lagna. The lagna/1st house of any *varga* is always a most significant area of the chart. Does it receive helpful or difficult aspects from other planets? What is the condition of its lord?

In the *Navamsha* chart a *vargottam* lagna (i.e. one that is identical to the lagna of the Rashi chart) strengthens the ability to positively project one's personality and to manifest all 1st house characteristics. This will be especially so if the lagna lord is also well placed in both charts.

Planets in angular or trinal houses (1,4,5,7,9 and 10) are considered strong and influential, while planets in dusthana houses (6, 8 or 12) are considered poorly placed and capable of causing difficulty or disappointment in relation to the affairs associated with that particular *varga*, particularly if they are with natural malefics or are in a weak sign.

CHAPTER TWELVE

THE VIMSHOTARI DASHA SYSTEM

"Then the Lord said, "My spirit shall not abide in man forever, for he is flesh, but his days shall be a hundred and twenty years." – *Genesis 6:3*

"O Brahmin! The full span of life for a human in Kali Yuga is said to be 120 years. Therefore, amongst the various Dasha systems Vimshotari Dasha is the prime dasha system."
– Brihat-Parashara-Hora-Shastra 46:15

There exist a variety of methods that enable the Jyotishi to understand how the birth chart unfolds its promise and potential during a person's life. The most widely used method is the *Vimshotari Dasha* system, also known as *Udu Dasha*. Sage Parashara, the great authority on Vedic astrology describes a variety of dasha systems (over 30) in his classic "Brihat-Parashara-Hora-Shastra," yet gives the greatest attention to expounding the *Vimshotari* system.

Maitreya said: "O supreme sage! You are omniscient and have infinite knowledge. Kindly be merciful and enlighten me in detail about the planetary dashas."

Maharishi Parashara said: "O Brahmin! You have asked a most appropriate question which will benefit one and all. I now unfold the secrets of the prevailing dasha systems. There are various types of dasha in use but for ordinary people Vimshotari dasha is the predominant one." *– Brihat-Parashara-Hora-Shastra 46:1-3*

Vimshotari means 120 and *Dasha* means a stage, condition, or period of life. Thus this *dasha* system covers a period of 120 years of life. *Vimshotari Dasha* is composed of 9 planetary periods or cycles *(dashas)* which vary between 6 and 20 years each.

Although always occurring in this order the exact starting point will be determined by the zodiacal position of the Moon at birth which, although described in terms of degrees and minutes of a sign, will always correspond to one of the Lunar *Nakshatras*.

Planet	Span of Years
Ketu	7
Venus	20
Sun	6
Moon	10
Mars	7
Rahu	18
Jupiter	16
Saturn	19
Mercury	17
Total	120

Nakshatra means a constellation or small group of stars. These are found by dividing the ecliptic into 27 equal segments of 13°20', beginning 0° Aries. The following list gives the number and name of each *Nakshatra*, followed by the area of the zodiac to which it corresponds and the planet which rules that particular *Nakshatra*.

Notice that the planets ruling the *Nakshatras* repeat their sequence three times. Thus each planet rules three *Nakshatras*. No one can convincingly explain just why the planets are arranged in this sequence or rule the number of years that they do. It remains an occult mystery.

The time span covered by each of the nine planets is known as its *mahadasha*. Each *mahadasha* is subdivided into nine subperiods or sub-cycles known as *bhuktis*. If the birth time was correctly recorded and

1	Ashwini	0°- 13°20' Aries	Ketu 7 years
2	Bharani	13°20' - 26°40' Aries	Venus 20 years
3	Krittika	26°40' Aries - 10° Taurus	Sun 6 years
4	Rohini	10° - 23°20' Taurus	Moon 10 years
5	Mrigashira	23°20' Taurus - 6°40' Gemini	Mars 7 years
6	Ardra	6°40' - 20° Gemini	Rahu 18 years
7	Punarvasu	20° Gemini - 3°20' Cancer	Jupiter 16 years
8	Pushya	3°20' - 16°40' Cancer	Saturn 19 years
9	Ashlesha	16°40' - 30° Cancer	Mercury 17 years
10	Magha	0°- 13°20' Leo	Ketu 7 years
11	Purva-Phalguni	13°20' - 26°40' Leo	Venus 20 years
12	Uttara-Phalguni	26°40' Leo - 10° Virgo	Sun 6 years
13	Hasta	10° - 23°20' Virgo	Moon 10 years
14	Chitra	23°20' Virgo - 6°40' Libra	Mars 7 years
15	Swati	6°40' - 20° Libra	Rahu 18 years
16	Vishakha	20° Libra - 3°20' Scorpio	Jupiter 16 years
17	Anuradha	3°20' -16°40' Scorpio	Saturn 19 years
18	Jyeshta	16°40' - 30° Scorpio	Mercury 17 years
19	Mula	0° - 13°20' Sagittarius	Ketu 7 years
20	Purvashadha	13°20' - 26°40' Sagittarius	Venus 20 years
21	Uttarashadha	26°40' Sagittarius -10° Capricorn	Sun 6 years
22	Shravana	10° - 23°20' Capricorn	Moon 10 years
23	Dhanishta	23°20' Capricorn - 6°40' Aquarius	Mars 7 years
24	Shatabhishak	6°40' - 20° Aquarius	Rahu 18 years
25	Purvabhadra	20° Aquarius - 3°20' Pisces	Jupiter 16 years
26	Uttarabhadra	3°20' - 16°40' Pisces	Saturn 19 years
27	Revati	16°40' - 30° Pisces	Mercury 17 years

accurately known then even the *bhuktis* can each be subdivided into nine smaller time periods known as *antardashas*. Thus the *mahadasha* of the Sun is composed of nine *bhuktis,* The first *bhukti* would be of the Sun itself, the second would be that of the Moon, the third would be of Mars, and so on—always following the same order as the *mahadasha* planets. The same sequence also applies to the *antardashas*.

In order to arrive at the *mahadasha* (period) and *bhukti* (sub-periods) operating at the time of birth you will need to make some calculations. Details of how the necessary calculations are made in order to establish the *dasha* balance at birth are given at the end of this section.

From here on we shall follow the common practice of referring to a *mahadasha* as a *dasha.* Also note, in some areas of India the *bhuktis* (sub-periods) are referred to as *antardashas* and the *antardashas* (sub-sub-periods) as *pratyantar-dashas* These differences of terminology should be born in mind when reading books on jyotish.

How to Calculate the Dashas

Although these days most astrologers use a computer program to make these calculations it is still useful to know how they are constructed and the method of making these calculations on paper. Many Indian Ephemerids and some books on Jyotish give tables for speedy calculation of dasha and bhuktis. Here we give an illustration of how the dashas are arrived at, taking as an example the dashas and bhuktis of John Lennon's chart.

First we take the position of the Moon at birth, which in John Lennon's case is 4°30' of Capricorn. By referring to the Nakshatra table at the beginning of this section you will find that the Moon is placed in the Nakshatra of Uttarashada which is ruled by the Sun. Therefore the dasha period at birth will be that of the Sun. If he had been born at the very beginning of Uttarashada (26°40' of Sagittarius) he would have the full 6 years of the Sun dasha to run. As this was not the case we have to calculate the exact point of the dasha into which he was born and determine how long it continued before changing to the next dasha.

To do this, we have first to convert the proper length of the Nakshatra (always 13°20') into minutes of space. As 60 = 1°, 13°20' = 800'.

Next we calculate the distance covered by the Moon in this particular Nakshatra. Uttarashada begins at 26°40' Sagittarius and ends a 10° Capricorn. As the Moon is placed in 4°30 minutes of Capricorn we know that the Moon has covered a distance of 7°50' in Uttarashada (3°20' of Sag. + 4°30' of Capricorn = 7°50'). This leaves another 5°30' of Uttarashad remaining to be traversed by the Moon. Converting 5°30' to minutes of space we find that the Moon has still to travel 330' of Uttarashada. At this point using a calculator will be helpful.

Divide the remaining distance by 800. 330 divided by 800 = 0.4125 which is the percentage of the period which remains between the Moon and the end of the Nakshatra. As the Sun dasha lasts for 6 years we multiply 0.4125 by 6. The result is 2.475 or 2 years and .475 months. Multiply .475 by 12 to get the months (.475 x 12 = 5.7). Multiply .7 by 30 to get the days (.7 x 30 = 21). Therefore 2 years 5 months and 21 days of the Sun dasha remains.

The date of John Lennon's birth was 9th October 1940 and the Moon in Uttarashada is ruled by the Sun. After 2 years 5 months and 21 days (1st April 1943) his Sun dasha ended and his Moon dasha begun. As the Moon dasha lasts exactly 10 years it ended on 1st April 1953 and the Mars dasha began. As the Mars dasha runs for 7 years, on the 1st April 1960 his Rahu dasha commenced.

Calculating the Bhuktis (Sub-periods)

The nine bhuktis of the main dasha period appear in the same order as the mahadashas. The first bhukti planet is always the same as the main dasha planet. Thus Rahu dasha always begins with Rahu bhukti, followed by Jupiter bhukti, then Saturn bhukti and so on. The lengths of the bhuktis are proportionate in length to the main dashas, as are the *antardashas*.

With the tabulation of the dasha and bhukti periods that follows it is a simple matter of counting back from the end of the first (birth) dasha in order to calculate the bhukti that was running at the time of birth and the number of days and months that had to elapse before the next one commenced.

Tables of Planetary Periods

Guidelines for Judging the Dashas

So how do we make use of the dashas and bhuktis?

"Whatever has been described here by way of planetary effects will occur in the planet's [maha]dasha, in its bhukti and in its antar[dasha]."

– Phaldeepika 21:1

Ketu Mahadasha – 7 years

Bhukti planet	Year	Month	Day
Ketu	0	4	27
Venus	1	2	0
Sun	0	4	6
Moon	0	7	0
Mars	0	4	27
Rahu	1	0	18
Jupiter	0	11	16
Saturn	1	1	9
Mercury	0	11	27

Venus Mahadasha – 20 years

Bhukti Planet	Year	Month	Day
Venus	3	4	0
Sun	1	0	0
Moon	1	8	0
Mars	1	2	0
Rahu	3	0	0
Jupiter	2	8	0
Saturn	3	2	0
Mercury	2	10	0
Ketu	1	2	0

Sun Mahadasha – 6 years

Bhukti Planet	Year	Month	Day
Sun	0	3	18
Moon	0	6	0
Mars	0	4	6
Rahu	0	10	24
Jupiter	0	9	18
Saturn	0	11	12
Mercury	0	10	6
Ketu	0	4	6
Venus	1	0	0

Moon Mahadasha – 10 years

Bhukti Planet	Year	Month	Day
Moon	0	10	0
Mars	0	7	0
Rahu	1	6	0
Jupiter	1	4	0
Saturn	1	7	0
Mercury	1	5	0
Ketu	0	7	0
Venus	1	8	0
Sun	0	6	0

Mars Mahadasha – 7 years

Bhukti Planet	Year	Month	Day
Mars	0	4	27
Rahu	1	0	18
Jupiter	0	11	6
Saturn	1	1	9
Mercury	0	11	27
Ketu	0	4	27
Venus	1	2	0
Sun	0	4	6
Moon	0	7	0

Rahu Mahadasha – 18 years

Bhukti Planet	Year	Month	Day
Rahu	2	8	12
Jupiter	2	4	24
Saturn	2	10	6
Mercury	2	6	18
Ketu	1	0	18
Venus	3	0	0
Sun	0	10	24
Moon	1	6	0
Mars	1	0	18

Jupiter Mahadasha – 16 years

Bhukti Planet	Year	Month	Day
Jupiter	2	1	18
Saturn	2	6	12
Mercury	2	3	6
Ketu	0	11	6
Venus	2	8	0
Sun	0	9	18
Moon	1	4	0
Mars	0	11	6
Rahu	2	4	24

Saturn Mahadasha – 19 years

Bhukti Planet	Year	Month	Day
Saturn	3	0	3
Mercury	2	8	9
Ketu	1	1	9
Venus	3	2	0
Sun	0	11	12
Moon	1	7	0
Mars	1	1	9
Rahu	2	10	6
Jupiter	2	6	12

Mercury Mahadasha – 17 years

Bhukti Planet	Year	Month	Day
Mercury	2	4	27
Ketu	0	11	27
Venus	2	10	0
Sun	0	10	6
Moon	1	5	0
Mars	0	11	27
Rahu	2	6	18
Jupiter	2	3	6
Saturn	2	8	9

The ability to accurately judge the development and outcome of someone's horoscope based on the dashas and bhuktis operating at any particular time is a skill that is acquired gradually and as a result of careful study and analysis.

The following essential guidelines should help you in acquiring the ability to judge the periods and subperiods with a fair degree of accuracy. Final conclusions should be arrived at only after comparing the dasha indications with the appropriate planetary transits.

Analyze the dasha results based upon the following:

Lordship: A dasha lord gives results according to houses over which it has lordship.

Position: A dasha lord will give results pertaining to the house in which it is placed.

Aspect and Conjunction: A dasha lord will give results modified by the nature of any planet that aspects or conjuncts it.

Dasha Results according to Planetary Strength

- If a planet is strong and well placed by sign it gives well-being and abundance in accordance with its nature.
- If a planet is weak (by house and sign) it contributes to poor health and lack of prosperity.
- If proceeding towards its point of debilitation *(avarohi)* its dasha inclines towards trouble and difficulty.
- If proceeding towards its point of exaltation *(aarohi)* its dasha inclines to be more auspicious.
- If a planet is well placed in the divisional charts (particularly the navamsha) its dasha proves even more beneficial.

During the dasha of a planet possessing directional strength (Jupiter and Mercury posses directional strength in the 1st house, Venus and the Moon in the 4th house, Saturn in the 7th and Sun and Mars in the 10th) the person will be successful in their ventures and will benefit from the direction indicated by the planet.

Dasha Results According to Planetary Position

- Any planet placed in a kendra (1st, 4th, 7th or 10th) or kona (5th or 9th) will prove fruitful.
- Any planet occupying the 6th, 8th or 12th house will tend to be harmful or troublesome. The dasha of a lord of the 6th, 8th or 12th house becomes beneficial if it is associated with a kona lord.
- The dasha of a natural benefic will fail to give good results if it is in the 3rd, 6th or 11th house. However, the dasha of a natural malefic, if placed in these houses, will prove helpful in that it will not manifest malefic results.
- The most benefic dasha is that of the lord of (a) kendra in a kona or associated with a kona lord, or (b) a kona lord placed in a kendra or associated with a kendra lord.
- The dashas of planets (a) posited in the 2nd or 7th houses (maraka houses), (b) associated with 2nd or 7th lords, or (c) placed in the 8th house, can indicate health problems or, if occurring at an appropriate time, indicate death.

Other Principal Considerations

The prime rule is to remember that whatever a planet indicates in the birthchart will be emphasized and highlighted during the planet's dasha.

The dasha of a debilitated lord of the 3rd, 6th, or 8th house, or the dasha of a debilitated planet posited in the 3rd, 6th, or 8th house, does not have the power to bring about the negative qualities associated with these houses.

During a planet's dasha all those things for which it is a karaka (representative) will become activated.

Any yogas in which the planet participates will become emphasized.

When a planet owns two houses, the house that contains its Moolatrikona sign will predominate. The effects of the other house will be less emphasized. Even so, matters associated with both houses will come to pass during the dasha period of the planet.

The house the planet owns that is first in sign sequence will tend to give its results during the first half of the dasha and the remaining house during the second half of the dasha. For example if someone has a chart with a Scorpio Ascendant, Saturn will rule the 3rd (Capricorn) and 4th (Aquarius) house. During the dasha of Saturn the first nine or so years would manifest matters more associated with 3rd house matters and the remaining years would be more associated with 4th house affairs. As the 4th house contains the moolatrikona sign the second half of the dasha will be much more significant and eventful.

The house occupied by the dasha lord's dispositor—the planet which owns the sign in which the dasha lord is placed—as well as the affairs of houses aspected by the dispositor, will also become activated.

No planet is entirely good or bad in its effects. Consider the natural tendencies of the planet as well as the qualities that it acquires due to house ownership of the chart under consideration.

Is the dasha lord in exaltation, own sign, friendly, neutral or enemy sign, or in its sign of fall? These factors will also have a decided influence on the manner in which it functions.

The dasha lord being retrograde or combust will also influence the manner in which it operates.

Rahu and Ketu

The dashas of Rahu and Ketu give the results of their dispositor (they act like the lords of the signs in which they are placed).

Rahu and Ketu also produce (a) the results appropriate to their intrinsic nature, (b) the effects of the house that they occupy, (c) the effects of any planet that conjoins or aspects them.

If Rahu or Ketu occupies a trine and is conjoined with the lord of an angle or if in an angle and conjoined by the lord of a trine this will give rise to a Raja Yoga which will manifest during the dasha of the Node concerned.

If they are placed in a kendra or trinal (kona) relationship to each other the period proves generally beneficial.

Apply the same guidelines when assessing the bhukti (sub-period) lord.

Judging The Interplay Between The Dasha And Bhukti Planets

Consider the compatibility of the two planets. Are they natural friends or enemies? What is their temporal relationship with each other? If the two planets are friends they will produce favorable results. If enemies they are more disruptive.

During a planet's dasha all matters associated with the house that it occupies and the houses that it rules and aspects will come into play. The signification of any planet with which the dasha lord has association will be brought out during the bhukti (subperiod) of the planet concerned. The bhukti planet will color and condition the manner in which the dasha lord functions.

Any aspect between the dasha and bhukti planets will bring noticeable results. If they mutually aspect each other the results will be even more emphasized.

Any type of *sambhanda* between the two planets gives added significance to their results.

Treat the sign containing the major period lord as the lagna and analyze the subperiod lord's position with respect to the major period lord, if the major period lord and the subperiod lord are placed $6^{th}/8^{th}$ or $2^{nd}/12^{th}$ to each other the period proves to be generally unfavorable as negative effects are more likely to be generated. If they are in an angular relationship to each other the results generated will be more dynamic. If they are in trinal houses to each other the results will be more favorable.

These are a few of the considerations which should be taken into account when learning to practice the predictive side of jyotish. Do not be daunted by the task. Develop your skills without undue haste. By testing them and mastering them one by one you will gain the necessary perspective on predictive chart interpretation.

An Example: John Lennon

There are several birth times given for John Lennon. This one set for 7 a.m. is the only one that makes sense when viewed through the lens of Vedic astrology. John's Rahu period began in 1960 and ended in 1978. Rahu is the most powerful planet in this chart as it occupies the same degree as the Ascendant point (17° Virgo). Rahu is in Virgo in the Rashi chart and in Gemini/1st house in the Navamsha. Both signs are highly favorable to Rahu, which was also moving from Stationary to Direct, another highly auspicious condition for Rahu. This brought him recognition, fame and wealth during Rahu dasha.

Rahu Mahadasha:	
Rahu Rahu	04/04/1960
Rahu Jup	12/16/1962
Rahu Sat	05/10/1965
Rahu Merc	03/17/1968
Rahu Ketu	10/03/1970
Rahu Ven	10/22/1971
Rahu Sun	10/22/1974
Rahu Moon	09/16/1975
Rahu Mars	03/16/1977
Jupiter Mahadasha:	
Jup Jup	04/04/1978
Jup Sat	05/23/1980

Ketu in the 7th house gave him a difficult marriage to Cynthia, his first wife, and an intense and somewhat obsessive relationship with Yoko. The interplay between Ketu in the 7th and Rahu in the 1st cause his Rahu period to be very turbulent. Ketu rules mindless and perception altering drugs and it was during Ketu bhukti of the Rahu dasha (the "Sgt. Pepper" period) that he became involved with experimenting with L.S.D.

John Lennon was shot in December 1980 during the Saturn bhukti of Jupiter dasha. Both planets are exactly conjunct and retrograde in the 8th house. They are also fully aspected by the 8th lord Mars—a highly inauspicious combination. Notice that bhukti lord Saturn is in Aries, the sign of its fall. Jupiter is lord of the 7th house and thus becomes a *maraka* (death inflicting) planet. Being retrograde caused it to lose many of its more positive qualities.

Short Guide to Dasha Results According to House Rulership

"Dashas manifest two types of results—general and distinctive. The natural characteristics of the planets cause the general results and the distinctive effects corresponds to their placement in the horoscope."

– Brihat-Parshara-Hora-Shastra 47:2

"If the lords and sub-lords occupy the 6th, 8th or 12th houses from each other they produce sorrow, distress and other kinds of difficulties."

– Sarvartha Chintamani 1:185

The following indications are equally applicable to both the main (mahadasha), subperiod (bhukti) and sub-subperiods (pratyantar) results. By "well placed" we mean that the planet concerned should be well placed by sign and house, receives benefic aspects and be free of malefic influences. By "weak" we mean that the planet is in the sign of its fall, aspected by malefics and devoid of benefic influences. In reality most planets will be somewhere between these extremes and the interpretation modified accordingly.

1st house
Well placed: The dasha of the lagna lord can bring increased power or authority, recognition and a feeling of general happiness or well-being.

Weak: lack of confidence and self-worth, misunderstanding by others, poor health.

2nd house

Well placed: Capable of bringing wealth or financial improvement. Happy and contented family life. Success in writing, teaching or lecturing.

Weak: The dasha of the 2nd lord can give health problems (due to the 2nd being a maraka house). Educational difficulties; financial problems: throat ailments. It may indicate difficulties for the spouse (being 8th from 7th).

3rd house

Well placed: The dasha of the 3rd lord can bring hidden talents to the surface. Fulfillment of desires. More energy and motivation. Can bring closer involvement with brothers and sisters or indicate benefits for them. Greater movement and short journeys. Success in the arts (theatre, music, dance etc.).

Weak: Difficulties achieving one's desires and ambitions. Lack of motivation. Problems involving brothers and sisters. Day to day plans and travel arrangements can be disrupted. Possibility of ailments involving the lungs or hearing.

4th house

Well placed: The dasha of the 4th lord can confer happiness, prosperity or vehicles. This is generally a good period for the native but may prove difficult for the father (8th from 9th). Benefits for or from one's mother. Good domestic conditions. Success in property dealings or moving home.

Weak: Problems with mother or difficulties for her. Problems with home or property. Lack of material comforts. Possible ailments involving the chest or stomach.

5th house

Well placed: The dasha of the 5th lord gives children. Inclines one to study or to express oneself more creatively. Good for focused spiritual practices. Elder brother or sister may get married (7th from 11th). Financial gains from investments. Greater optimism and mental clarity. Help from others. Generally a more creative and enjoyable period of one's life.

Weak: Problems with children. Financial losses from investments or speculative ventures. General lack of success. Can feel depressed or uncertain about one's future. Possible health problems involving the back or heart.

6th house

Well placed: The dasha of the 6th lord brings greater stamina to resist difficulties and to overcome problems associated with the 6th house. Health improves or one develops healing skills. It arouses one's competitive tendencies. Happiness in one's job or daily work. Favorable for the father (10th from 9th house).

Weak: Gives rise to a variety of difficulties. Can indicate trouble from opponents or competitors, disease (health problems indicated by the planet ruling or occupying the 6th), accident or debt.

7th house

Well placed: The dasha of the 7th lord can, if appropriate, indicate marriage or the commencement of a long term relationship. Favorable for business partnerships and for obtaining new position or public prominence. Favorable for an expansion of business, especially if this involves dealings with the public (7th is the house of "others").

Weak: Difficulties in establishing long term relationships, difficult romantic involvement, marital problems or possible divorce. Could be difficult for health (a maraka lord).

8th house

Well placed: The dasha of the 8th lord may bring financial gains from wills, legacies or unexpected sources. Financial gains arising from one's spouse or business partner. This dasha may also arouse past life habits and tendencies. It inclines one towards internalized or secretive psychic or occult involvement and sometimes there is a greater attraction towards ideas or situations that are non-traditional or unorthodox. Spiritual interests can be aroused or spiritual endeavours and experiences can be intensified. Can give rise to involvement in controversy. This dasha tends to bring changes to the native's life pattern.

Weak: The more hidden areas of ones life may be revealed. Problems with joint finances. Difficulties in receiving due payment from others. Unforeseen danger, accidents, long-term ailments or, if other indications are supportive, even death can be indicated. Ailments may involve the reproductive system.

9th house

Well placed: The dasha of the 9th lord inclined one to perform acts of charity and to perform religious duties such as undertaking a pilgrimage or performing religious rituals. Good for spiritual practices and gaining higher knowledge. May meet one's guru. Increase in religious or devotional endeavours. Enjoyable travel to other countries. Often a lucky period. A favorable time for the father and/or one's relationship with him. Birth of children is also possible (5th from 5th).

Weak: Problems with one's spiritual endeavours. Lack of faith or belief in higher realities. Difficulties while travelling abroad. One's mother may develop health problems. (6th from 4th). Lack of good fortune.

10th house

Well placed: The dasha of the 10th lord gives greater status or wealth. Can be a period of professional excellence or expansion of career. Good for gaining favours from authorities, government or official bodies. Good for public recognition and for gaining honours or awards for one's endeavors. A time in which one can gain increased power and influence in the world.

Weak: Problems with those in authority. Difficulties with one's public standing, professional life or career prospects.

11th house

Well placed: The dasha of the 11th lord can increases income, can indicate job promotion or give general gains. Realization of important goals or ambitions. Beneficial time for relationship with elder brothers and sisters. Formation of new friendships or benefits from friends. Offspring may get married (7th from 5th).

Weak: Failure to realize goals and ambitions. Failure of projects. Missed opportunities. Difficult for relationship with elder siblings or a problematic time for them. Possibility of accidents (6th from 6th). Could be bad for the mother (8th from 4th).

12th house

Well placed: One may invest money in various projects. Sexual experiences or enjoyment may become more emphasized. May develop foreign connections or travel to distant lands. Good for spiritual development as this house is associated with enlightenment and liberation. One may reside in a monastery or ashram, or live a very secluded life.

Weak: Unexpected expenses or debts. The dasha of the 12th lord often incurs some kind of loss or expenditure. Danger of confinement, hospitalization or imprisonment. Problems due to theft or other criminal activities. Ailments could involve the feet or be associated with one's sight or hearing. Generally not good for overall health and robustness.

These are just a few possibilities and the list could easily be amplified. Sensitivity, experience and common sense are needed in applying the indications of Vimshotari Dasha. It is never safe (or ethical) to give predictions to anyone unless some background and details about the lifestyle of that person has been obtained. The purpose of an astrological reading should always be to help, inspire and uplift the client, not to alarm them unnecessarily or try and impress the client with your skill.

CHAPTER THIRTEEN

TRANSITS

There are a number of methods of viewing and understanding the manner in which a birth chart unfolds. The four most important systems in use are:

<u>One Day for One Year</u> *(Dina Varsha Paddhati)* This system is now mainly used by Western Astrologers although versions of it are also found in branches of Indian Astrology.

<u>Solar Revolutions</u> *(Tajika Paddhati)* used in both Western and Indian astrology, although the Indian method is more elaborate.

<u>Transits</u> *(Gochara Paddhati)* Used in nearly all astrologies.

<u>Planetary Periods</u> *(Dasha Paddhati)* The various dasha systems are used exclusively by Vedic Astrologers.

In the last chapter we studied the most popular and important of the dasha systems—Vimshottari dasha. In this chapter we examine planetary transits.

A transit refers to the passage of a planet through the zodiac at a particular point in time. The constantly changing planetary positions (transits) are used in reference to the birth chart or horoscope, which depicts a diagram of planetary positions frozen in time and space. A transit chart can be created with reference to the birth chart in order to observe the relationship between the two charts. The transit chart will indicate those planets and areas of the birth chart that are being activated by the transit chart.

When using transits it is usually the current position in the sky of the planets that are being used in order to understand the influences affecting one's life. In order to do this you will need an Ephemeris (a publication giving the daily position of the planets). It is not usually necessary to draw a separate transit chart. The transits of the relevant planets can simply be noted or recorded in pencil around the outside of the birth chart.

As an example, let us suppose that the current position of Jupiter is found to coincide with the rising degree of your Ascendant. The likelihood is that you will be feeling more optimistic than usual. Agreeable circumstances are more likely to be encountered and so on. Throughout the 12 month period that Jupiter takes to transit your Ascendant sign you will tend to experience the influence of the planet on your general outlook on life. Matters associated with the house position of Jupiter and the houses that it rules in your birth chart will make some sort of impact on your life.

Of course, we should consider the positions of all the planetary transits—not just one in isolation. Perhaps at the same time that Jupiter is in your 1st house transiting Saturn is passing through your 10th house, indicating that this is also a time when you find yourself having to pay greater attention to your career—perhaps there are added responsibilities in the workplace. In this way we can build up a picture of your current situation and circumstances.

Transits, just like dashas, will never contradict the basic indications of the birth chart. They only serve to help us understand when the potentials indicated in the natal chart are likely to manifest. Dashas and transits are tools for determining the correct timing of horoscopic factors.

Most classical writers as well as a few modern practitioners of Jyotish, calculate the results of transit with reference to the Moon-sign of the birth chart rather than from the Ascendant. In practice it will be found that this technique does not give such reliable results. Transit influences should be considered primarily in relation to the Ascendant. If used at all, the Moon sign Ascendant should be used in a subordinate role.

The most pronounced effects of a transiting planet occur at the time that it comes into conjunction or opposition with a planet in the natal chart. When this takes place the natal planet (planet in the birth chart) is stimulated into action through the qualities represented by the transiting planet. If the transiting planet is fast moving then the effect is hardly noticeable or is influential for only a short while. The slower moving planets have a greater long term influence and are thus the ones generally given more consideration. The following table gives the average duration of the passage of a planet through a sign.

Planet	Approximate Duration in a Sign
Moon	Just over 2 & 1/4 days
Sun	1 month
Mercury	Similar to the Sun (but more variable)
Venus	Similar to the Sun (but more variable)
Mars	Nearly 2 months (55 days)
Jupiter	1 year
Saturn	Nearly 2 & 1/2 years
Rahu/Ketu	1 year 7 months
Uranus	7 years
Neptune	Nearly 18 years
Pluto	Just over 20 years

You will have noticed that the outer planets (Uranus, Neptune and Pluto) have also been included in the above table. Because they are so distant and slow moving they only create an impact as transits when in close conjunction or opposition to natal planets, or form a 90° angle to them. Their sign/house transits should be disregarded. This does not apply to the two most important transiting planets—Jupiter and Saturn.

Besides being innately significant, when they form an exact conjunction with a natal planet, transiting Jupiter and Saturn have an impact on the houses which they are passing through. They also form drishti aspect just as they do as natal planets. This is also true of Mars. The faster transiting planets, the Moon, Sun and Venus, are usually only significant in their conjunctions with natal planets. In their cases, the influence will only last for a couple of days, or in the case of the Moon for a few hours (the exception being when there is a conjunction from a Full or New Moon, which is of greater important and can be influential for up to a week).

It is important to check the speed of a transiting planet from the Ephemeris as this is a variable factor. If the transiting planet is retrograde, our understanding of its influence can be adjusted accordingly.

If it is stationary (as it will be for a short period when changing from direct to retrograde or from retrograde back to direct) then its impact is greater.

Transits of the Sun and Moon: These should be used together as the positions of Sun, Earth and Moon are jointly responsible for creating the Full and New Moons, which are the only phases of the lunar transits worth noting. Eclipses sometimes occur at such times and these make a much greater impact.

An eclipse of the Sun takes place at New Moon (the conjunction of the Sun and Moon). This occurs when the latter has no latitude, so that not only are they both on the same degree of the ecliptic but also in line with each other as seen from the Earth.

An eclipse of the Moon takes place at Full Moon (an opposition between the Sun and Moon) when the Moon is again without latitude, with the Earth placed between the two.

If an eclipsed Sun or Moon conjunct any natal planets it is considered ominous or disruptive because the Nodes will be in conjunction with the Sun and/or the Moon. An eclipse can also effect the house of the natal chart in which it occurs.

A Solar Eclipse is far more powerful than a New Moon, usually signifying dramatic new developments caused by its powerful energizing influence on the house or planet concerned. A Full Moon is less powerful in its impact than a New Moon but is more important when it occurs as a Lunar Eclipse.

Transits of Mercury: These are rarely of great importance. Mercury transits can relate to communications, meetings, journeys or undertakings. A retrograde Mercury will often delay such things.

Transits of Venus: Brings harmonious and pleasant experiences. Meeting with loved ones is sometimes indicated.

Transits of Mars: Gives an urge towards action. Tends to disrupt the established rhythm of life. Energizes the planet/house that it passes through or aspects.

Transits of Jupiter: Gives an urge to expand into new areas of experience. Attunes one to future possibilities. Often indicates increased abundance or good fortune. In some cases it can indicate exaggeration or excessiveness.

Transits of Saturn: Stabilizes, delays or slows down. Brings a practical or constricting influence to the planet which it contacts and the house through which it passes.

Transits of Rahu and Ketu: Rahu's transit can give desires and obsessions associated with the planet it conjuncts or with the affairs of house through which it transits. Ketu can awaken fears, phobias or obsessions. On the positive side it can have a spiritually uplifting influence.

Transits of Uranus: Hastens change. Speeds up or disrupts the affairs of the planet with which it comes into contact.

Transits of Neptune: Sensitizes, refines, dissolves or brings deception to affairs of the planet over which it transits. The negative side of Neptune can cause vagueness, fantasy, muddle, nebulousness and a fear of facing practical issues.

Transits of Pluto: Brings things to the surface so that they may undergo transformation. It frequently removes old or obsolete situations or circumstances in order that new patterns of life may emerge.

The three outer planets, Uranus, Neptune and Pluto, are capable of causing long term changes to our circumstances and outlook on life.

The description of these transits have deliberately been kept brief as they are capable of so many variations. It is important to remember that the transiting planet cannot contradict the fundamental indications of the birth-chart, a common mistake for beginners to make which often leads to the prediction of situations that fail to materialize.

"...be considerate and expound a system of study for the persons who would be having slow perceptions and through which they could gain a clear knowledge about their happiness, sorrows and longevity merely by delineating the positions of the planets in transit." – *Brihat Parasara Hora Shastra 68.4*

Guidelines to Interpreting Transits

The full range of natal qualities associated with a planet have the potential to manifest during its transit through the birth chart. However, it is important to keep in mind that a transiting planet will color and influence the qualities of the natal planet or house that it is transiting or aspecting—not the other way around. Natal planets do not modify the behavior of transiting planets but transiting planets do modify behavior of natal planets.

A most important guideline to using transits is to coordinate them with the dashas and bhuktis. Suppose one is in Jupiter dasha—Venus bhukti. During this period the transits of Jupiter and Venus will be particularly significant. Even the house and sign that Venus is transiting, although not normally influential, will have an added significance in understanding Venus bhukti because the results of the current bhukti depend to a large extent upon the transit strength of the bhukti lord. However, transits do not usually have the capacity to override or contradict the indications of the dasha or bhukti in which they occur.

Planets that are weak in the natal chart create problems when transited by strong malefics and will not be fully receptive to or capable of responding to the uplifting influence of benefics.

Conversely, strong natal planets that are benefics will tend to have greater resistance to transiting malefics, while strong natal malefics are unlikely to respond well to transiting benefics.

A weak natal planet, during its bhuktis, will not be so capable of protecting or promoting the matters associated with the houses ruled by it irrespective of the current transit strength of that weak planet.

For a quick assessment of current transit influences you can focus upon the house positions and aspects of transiting Jupiter and Saturn. This will be found to be basic but practical and effective.

Traditional Jyotish gives emphasis to the passage of transits through the houses of the natal chart, whereas modern Western astrology places much more emphasis on the conjunction, opposition (180°) and square (90°) aspects created by transits to natal planets and to angles such as the Ascendant and M.C. In our opinion both approaches give significant results.

When judging the duration of a transit influence, a transiting planet forming a conjunction with a natal planet will manifest its influence most strongly when 1° away from the natal planet. This influence will decline once it separates from the natal planet by a distance of 1°.

"Saturn is the supreme terrifier among planets. All beings fear him, for he rules bereavements and misfortunes. If pleased he will give you a kingdom, but if irate he will snatch everything away from you in a moment."
– *The Greatness of Saturn, Robert Svoboda*

Sade Sati

The period in which Saturn transits the Moon is generally considered to be a difficult one, capable of lowering one's energy, slowing down the pace of life, generating a more pessimistic or negative outlook on life and causing a marked dip in one's normal emotional buoyancy.

In India it is believed that not only is Saturn's transit of the whole of one's Moon sign most inauspicious, but that even the presence of Saturn transiting the adjacent signs is capable of bringing difficult conditions into one's life. Saturn takes two and a half years to transit any sign. The effects are said to be slow and ponderous. *Sade Sati* means "seven and a half" and refers to the seven and a half year period that it takes for Saturn to transit the sign containing the Moon as well as the signs either side of the Moon.

Although no reference to *Sade Sati* is to be found in the classical jyotish texts *Sade Sati* is nevertheless widely feared throughout India. Every Indian will know what *Sade Sati* refers to. It's an established part of Hindu folk lore.

In practice, the transit of Saturn through one's Moon sign is likely to make its presence felt even in adjacent signs. Provided it is within 12 degrees of a conjunction with the Moon, one is likely to experience its impact. Otherwise one can safely ignore the dreaded *Sade Sati*.

From what has been said regarding *Sade Sati* and the use of the Moon sign as an ascendant for transits, it would seem that our ancestors were much more sensitive to lunar influences than we are today—some cultures still are. However, when using Jyotish in our present day western culture we should be cautious about placing too much emphasis on *Sade Sati* or on transits as counted from the Moon sign.

Maturity of Planets

All planets in the birth chart take time to reach their point of maturity—a time when they are capable of becoming truly functional in the horoscope. Once a planet has reached its year of maturity, the matters represented by the houses that it owns will also be of greater significance to the individual and the house in which it is placed will be more pronounced in its influence on the person's life. This influence will continue for a period of about 12 months and will be particularly noticeable in the case of one's ruling planet and of the strongest planet in the chart.

The following table shows the year in which the planets reach their maturity. If the planet is prominent in the birth chart then its influence becomes more pronounced, independently of whether or not that particular planet is emphasized by transit or dashas.

Planetary Ages

The following tables give the periods in one's life to which particular planets form a background influence. They are overridden by the dashas and transits as well is the times of planetary maturity given above. The planetary ages are best used when one has a birth chart but no dasha or transit information.

Planet	Age of Maturation		Planet	Period of Life
Jupiter	15 years (15 to 16)		Moon	0 to 4
Sun	21 years (21 to 22)		Mercury	5 to 14
Moon	23 years (23 to 24)		Venus	15 to 22
Venus	24 years (24 to 25)		Sun	23 to 41
Mars	27 years (27 to 28)		Mars	42 to 56
Mercury	31 years (31 to 32)		Jupiter	57 to 68
Saturn	35 years (35 to 36)		Saturn	68 to 108
Rahu	41 years (41 to 42)			
Ketu	47 years (47 to 48)			

For example, if Venus is poorly placed in the natal chart but the Sun is well placed, success or happiness in the person's life will be unlikely until the age of 23. A weak Mars and a strong Jupiter indicate lack of success or initiative until ones late 50's. May your Mars be strong!

CHAPTER FOURTEEN

JYOTISH AND AYURVEDA

Since ancient times the study of Jyotish and Ayurveda have been practiced as complementary disciplines. Ayurveda is the traditional Indian healing system that is gaining increasing popularity in the Western world. The word Ayurveda means "knowledge of life."

One important contribution of Ayurveda is the classification of people according to their constitutional type. Once this classification is established, the diagnosis and treatment of a person can be correctly determined.

There are three basic constitutions, or *doshas*, which arise out of the five elements (earth, water, fire, air and ether). Earth and water give rise to Kapha, Fire gives rise to Pitta and when air combines with ether it gives rise to Vata.

Typical Characteristics of the Doshas

Kapha types: are of a calm and thoughtful disposition. They have well developed bodies. They have good appetites, eat well and enjoy their food, but have a tendency to put on weight. Their bones, tendons and veins are not prominent. Their complexion is often fair or pale and their skin tends to be moist, soft and cold to the touch. Hair is usually thick, dark, and soft. Sleep tends to be sound. Kapha people may be slow in their movements but they have good endurance and plenty of stamina.

Psychologically they are tolerant, calm and have forgiving natures. On the negative side they can be possessive, greedy and attached to material values or objects. Although comprehension can be slow, once understood knowledge is well retained.

Pitta types: tend to have plenty of energy and enjoy an active life. Their skin is normally soft and the complexion possesses a good color although it may be flushed. Hair has a tendency towards early greying and/or baldness. Vision tends to be poor. Pitta people have strong appetite and good digestion. The body temperature tends to be high and their hands usually feel warm. They perspire freely and have a low tolerance of heat and sunlight.

Psychologically Pitta people are intelligent and have goods powers of comprehension. They are often ambitious to get ahead. Negatively they can be somewhat hot-headed, argumentative and impulsive.

Vata types: Tend to be tall and slim, usually with emphasized joints, veins and muscles. Skin is dry and cold, nails are usually brittle and the hair dry and scant. They feel the cold more easily than other types. Vata people talk fast and have rapid movements. They tend to be creative, active and alert but are often anxious and restless. Their appetite is variable and they tend to eat quickly and irregularly. They find difficulty in establishing regular habits or routines and they can easily become tired. Sleep patterns can be irregular or easily disturbed.

Psychologically they are quick to comprehend but have short memories. Will-power tends to be weak and anxiety levels tend to be high. They are mentally sensitive and can easily become stressed and fearful.

Any good book on Ayurveda will give a more detailed profile of these three types. Of course very few people correspond perfectly to one of them. Most of us are a combination of all three doshas, but generally one dosha is predominating over the others. Sometimes two doshas will be emphasized and the third will be weak—the combinations are manifold.

When the natural balance of our doshas becomes disturbed we experience discomfort or ill health. By understanding the factors which cause this imbalance and the dosha(s) most responsible for giving rise to the disturbance, steps can be taken to restore the natural harmony and balance of our constitution—our *Prakruti.*

The Vedic birth chart can play an important role in establishing one's natural constitution *(prakruti),* indicating the aggravating dosha(s) and particular constitutional weaknesses. The table below classifies the elements, signs and planets associated with each dosha. Some signs and planets are capable of representing two different doshas. Mercury is sometimes classified as *tridosha* (representing all the doshas) due to its variable nature.

	VATA	PITTA	KAPHA
Element	Air	Fire	Earth & Water
Planets			
Primary Planets	Saturn, Mercury, Rahu	Sun, Mars, Ketu	Moon, Venus, Jupiter
Secondary	Venus (K&P)	Jupiter (K&P)	Saturn (V&K)
Outer Planets	Uranus (Merc. octave)	Pluto (Mars octave)	Neptune (Venus octave)
Signs			
Primary	Gemini	Aries	Taurus
General	Virgo	Leo	Cancer
Mixed	Libra (V&K) Aquarius (V&P)	Sag. (P&K) Scorpio (P&K)	Pisces (K&P) Capricorn (K&V)

K = Kapha; P = Pitta: V = Vata.

Determination of Dosha

The most important consideration in determining the individuals natural constitution is the Ascendant and 1st house (physical type). You should examine the nature of Ascending sign, *including* the nature of any planets in the 1st house and of any planets aspecting the 1st house.

Next you should examine the ruling planet, while taking into consideration modification due to its sign placement, as well as any planets which may conjoin or aspect it.

Both the Sun and the Moon should also be examined. The Sun because it is the natural karaka, or significator, for the 1st house and the Moon, not only because it represents our emotional/mental nature but also because it gives shape and sustenance to all earthly matters. It is useful to give somewhat more emphasis to the Sun for men and to the Moon for women.

The strongest planet in the horoscope is also an important consideration.

At this point it would be useful to follow through these ideas using an example chart:

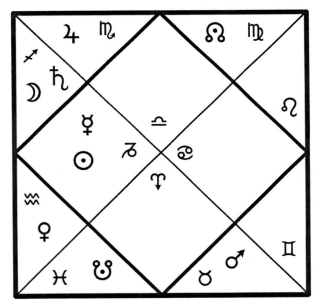

Here we have a Libra Ascendant/1st house, indicating someone who has natural Vata tendencies. There are no planets in the 1st house nor are there any aspects being cast on the ascendant. Next we examine the ruling planet. This is Venus, which occupies Aquarius (reinforcing the Vata influence). It is aspected by Saturn, another Vata influence.

The Sun, which is the natural karaka for the 1st house, is in Capricorn (Kapha) although this is modified by the presence of Mercury (Vata).

The Moon is in Sagittarius (Pitta) but does not have a great deal of strength (paksha bala). It's natural Kapha qualities are therefore easily modified by the presence of Saturn (Vata) and the aspect of Mars (Pitta).

So far we have a constitution that is predominantly Vata, with Kapha and Pitta as secondary influences. Of the two secondary influences Kapha is a little more predominant than Pitta.

Now we should examine the 6th house because of its association with health issues, disease tendencies, and general digestive powers. The planet ruling this house, planets occupying it, along with aspects cast or received, are all important considerations when establishing factors which <u>disrupt</u> the health and balance of the doshas.

If we look at the example chart we find that Jupiter rules the 6th house (through Pisces) and is also aspecting it. A planet aspecting its own sign benefits the house, no damage is done by this aspect. However the presence of Ketu in the 6th does create difficulties. Ketu in the 6th causes problems that are usually subtle or difficult to diagnose— sometimes manifesting as psychic disturbances.

Vata is the least stable of the doshas and in this example it is easily disturbed and unbalanced by Pitta, caused by Ketu (Pitta) being in the 6th house and Mars (Pitta) aspecting the 6th lord (Jupiter) from the 8th house.

Add to this the fact that a weak Moon (*manas*, the mind) is associated with Saturn and aspected by Mars and it will come as no surprise that this person has suffered terribly with irrational fears and anxieties which have disturbed her peace of mind and caused insomnia for years. All these are symptoms of disturbed Vata.

"When aggravated, Vata affects the strength, complexion, happiness and life span. It excites the mind and strikes the senses. It gives grief, fear, confusion, humility and delirium." – *The Charaka Samhita 12.8*

We have said that the strongest planet should also be taken into consideration. In this case the Sun should be considered strong by virtue of being in a kendra (angular house). Association with Mercury damages it because Mercury rules the difficult 12th house that contains Rahu (Vata). Thus Rahu's energy is carried with Mercury, and Mercury carries

12th house/Rahu qualities to the Sun, already a difficult planet for a Libra Ascendant due to ownership of the 11th house.

Medical Astrology

The birth chart can also assist in determining the basic health of a person, regardless of what their constitutional type may happen to be according to Ayurveda. This enables us to use Vedic astrology as an aid to medical diagnosis, no matter what the medical system to which we may be relating the chart. The chart provides information on (a) the overall strength and vitality of the body, (b) longevity, (c) likely areas of the body and body systems that are vulnerable to weakness or disease and (d) any tendency towards psychological problems. It can also gauge the duration of a disease through the study of transits and dashas.

To determine the overall health of a person, we give particular attention to the Ascendant, the ruling planet and the Sun (karaka of the 1st house) as these are the factors which represent the strength and vitality of the physical body.

Next we examine the 6th house and its lord because these factors indicate the person's potential for disease and their susceptibility to health problems.

We also examine the 8th and 12th houses and their lords. The 8th house represents longevity and the potential for chronic or longterm illness (also severe accidents and injuries). The 12th house should be studied for indications of longterm confinement or hospitalization.

Although of secondary importance the 11th and 3rd houses can also be examined in the same way as the 6th and 8th.

To gain further insight, use the Navamsha chart alongside the Rashi chart. Other divisional charts that can be used in relation to medical astrology are the Drekkana, Dwadamsha and Trimsamsa charts. The Drekkana chart indicates vitality while the Dwadamsha indicates hereditary traits and can indicate hereditary illnesses or weaknesses. The Trimsamsa chart indicates planets that are likely to be very difficult or harmful.

Importance of the Rashi Chart

In determining the degree of health or sickness that a person is likely to encounter it is of primary importance to examine the overall indications of the birth chart in relation to the Ascendant. Benefics will do good if located in angles or trines (1st, 4th, 5th, 7th, 9th and 10th) Benefics in the 5th house are more capable of benefiting the health than those located in the 9th. Malefics occupying these positions are capable of damaging the health. Malefics in Upachaya houses (3rd, 6th, 10th and 11th) are capable of improving over the course of time. Benefics in Dusthanas (6th, 8th, or 12th) are weakened in their ability to give positive effects. The 2nd and 7th house lords have the potential to be harmful as these become maraka lords.

Any benefic planet aspecting the Ascendant will be good for the health. Any malefic planet aspecting the Ascendant can harm the health. Natural benefics on either side of the Ascendant (or the Moon) fortify one's health. Malefics occupying these positions will have the reverse effect.

The body will have good resistance to disease if the Ascendant is *vargottama* (the same in both the Rashi and the Navamsha). A *vargottama* Ascendant lord is also a strengthening factor.

Provided they are not retrograde or afflicted, natural benefics can contribute to good health provided they are located in angles and trines. Several angular benefics will greatly strengthen a person's health, enabling them to overcome afflictions shown elsewhere in the chart. However, retrograde benefics are much weakened and rendered more unreliable. If poorly placed by sign position or aspected by malefics, their ability to fortify the health is again weakened although they may still be of some benefit. Combustion with the Sun does not generally weaken the health unless within a degree or so of an exact conjunction.

Of the natural benefics Jupiter is the best for health and Venus is second. Mercury is third in strength and only really helpful if in association with another benefic. The position, power, strength, and the quality of the Moon should be carefully assessed. Is it waxing or waning? Is it near or distant from the Sun? Does it own difficult houses such as the 6th, 8th or 12th? All of these considerations will determine whether it has a negative or positive impact upon one's health. For example, an afflicted Moon aspecting the Ascendant from the 7th house (a maraka house) will be causing more harm than good.

Because the 7th house is a maraka house as well as an angular house, and because planets in the 7th directly aspect the 1st House/Ascendant, it is particularly difficult to have malefics here. The Rahu-Ketu axis falling in $1^{st}/7^{th}$ houses can be detrimental to the health. Saturn placed here depletes one's energy and vitality and Mars can give susceptibility to toxic infections, inflammation or fever.

Remember to take note of the Ascendant ruler. If it associates with or aspects a natural benefic, particularly Jupiter, the overall health of the person is benefited. The reverse is true when the Ascendant ruler associates with a natural malefic, particularly Saturn. A debilitated Ascendant lord (in its fall or in the sign of a great enemy) can increase one's susceptibility to disease. If in its exaltation or own sign one is likely to have good vitality and greater immunity to disease.

Any association between the Ascendant lord and the lords of the 6th, 8th and 12th houses can give rise to health problems.

Both the signs and the houses are associated with different areas of the body. Memorizing the following table will help in health assessments. If a sign or house is occupied by malefic planets the associated regions of the body tend to suffer. Thus if malefics occupy the 2nd house as well as Taurus the throat, neck or shoulders will be weak areas of the body. If both the 3rd house and Gemini are afflicted then one suffers with lung problems.

Sign	House	Area of Body
Aries	1st House	Head, brain, eyes, front of head down to eyes and back of head down to base of skull.
Taurus	2nd House	Neck, face, the upper neck to the larynx and the back of the neck to the shoulder, including the cerebellum.
Gemini	3rd House	Upper chest, including the lungs, the shoulders and the upper arms.
Cancer	4th House	Breast, and the front part of the chest to the border of the ribs and elbows, including the stomach.
Leo	5th House	Solar Plexus region and the mid and upper back, including the small intestines, as well as body vitality in general via the heart.
Virgo	6th House	Hands. Navel Region. Mid-abdomen, including the colon. Digestive system generally, also body health as a whole.
Libra	7th House	Lower Abdomen and lumbar region, including the kidneys and internal genitalia.
Scorpio	8th House	Pubic region. Sacrum, rectum, bladder, lower back, hips and thighs.
Sagittarius	9th House	Thighs, hips as well as and lower back. Also governs the arteries.
Capricorn	10th House	Knees. Besides the knees it also governs the bones and joints of the entire body.
Aquarius	11th House	Calves and the skin. Besides these it also governs the power of exhalation.
Pisces	12th House	Feet. Besides the feet it also governs the lymphatic system.

The Sun represents bone, the Moon represents blood, Mars represent muscle, Mercury represents the skin, Jupiter represents fat, Venus represents semen and urine and Saturn represents the nerves. Whichever planet rules the Ascendant will emphasize the importance of the corresponding tissue/body system.

If a planet occupies the Ascendant sign/1st house then tissues associated with that planet become all the more emphasized. If there is any association or aspect from malefic planets to the Ascendant lord or 1st house, then the tissue associated with the malefic will be vulnerable to disease or damage.

In the same way, if the lord of the ascendant is weak or in some way associated with malefic planets, then there will be a weakness in the organs of the body represented by the Ascendant sign.

If you are interested in exploring Medical Astrology in more detail you will find *Essentials of Medical Astrology* and *Subtleties of Medical Astrology*, both by Dr. K. S. Charak, to be informative and well written books.

"One should choose as a livelihood, those activities which are consistent with dharma (that which upholds nature and society), adhere to the path of peace, and engage in studies to acquire useful knowledge. This is the way to happiness."
 – *Charaka Samhita*

CHAPTER FIFTEEN

REMEDIAL MEASURES

Gemstone or Mantra

When a planet is weak or afflicted in the birth chart there are a variety of measures that can be taken to strengthen or balance the energy and qualities of that planet. The most frequently used remedial measures are the wearing of a gemstone or the regular recitation of a planetary mantra (a sequence of sounds that have a vibrational influence that modifies the manner in which a planets energy becomes manifest).

Although appropriate planetary mantras are safe to use, they require some time and attention to their practice. For this reason many people will go for the easy option—wearing a gemstone. The problem with a gemstone, whether worn as an astrological ring or as a pendant, is that it enhances the energy of a planet for better or for worse. Thus a weak planet will have its strength increased by wearing the appropriate gemstone but this can do more harm than good if the planet owns difficult houses. By referring to the chapter on Ascendants you will be able to ascertain which planets are beneficial and which are malefic for a particular Ascendant. If a planet is classified as a benefic for a particular Ascendant it's gemstone can be safely worn. *Never wear the gemstone of a planet that has a malefic relationship to the Ascending sign.*

The gemstone of the planet ruling your ascendant can be worn throughout your life as it will have a strengthening influence on the body, vitality, and other 1st house indications. Other appropriate stones can be worn on a long term basis or for the duration of the planets dasha. Wearing gemstones can be an expensive business but need not be so. Gemstones should be of a high quality and free of serious imperfections.

Planet	Gemstone	Substitute	Setting	Hand	Finger
Sun	Ruby	Garnet	Gold (Silver)	Right	Ring
Moon	Pearl	Moonstone	Silver/White Gold	Left	Ring or Index
Mars	Red Coral	Carnelian, Red Jasper	Silver or Copper & Gold	Right	Index or Ring
Mercury	Emerald	Peridot	Gold or Silver	Either	Little
Jupiter	Yellow Sapphire	Yellow Topaz, Citrine	Gold	Right	Index
Venus	Diamond	White Sapphire, Clear Quartz	White Gold or Silver	Left	Middle or Little
Saturn	Blue Sapphire	Amethyst	Gold or Silver	Either	Middle
Rahu	Hessonite Garnet	Golden Grossularite	Gold or Silver	Either	Middle or Little
Ketu	Cat's Eye	Quartz Cat's Eye	Silver or White Gold	Either	Middle or Little

Appropriate Gemstone Recommendations

Therefore, if you decide to go for the primary gemstone it is likely to be an expensive purchase. For this reason there are certain secondary or substitute stones that are less costly but can be equally effective. These are generally worn in the form of a pendant or necklace as their recommended size can often make them impractical to be worn as astrological rings.

There are several important points to keep in mind when planning to wear an astrological gemstone. One is that the stone must be in contact with the skin, the other is that the time that the stone is first worn permanently, and is governed by certain astrological considerations.

Fingers of the hand and their relation to the elements and planets:

Index finger	Ether	Jupiter, Moon, Mars
Middle finger	Air	Saturn, Venus, (Rahu, Ketu).
Ring finger	Fire, Water	Sun, Moon, Mars (Ketu)
Little finger	Earth	Mercury, Venus. (Rahu, Ketu).

The thumb, although related to Mars and the fire element, is not used for astrological rings. The index finger (next to the thumb) is ruled by Jupiter, the middle finger by Saturn, the ring finger by the Sun and the little finger by Mercury. The Moon and Venus are related to areas of the palm so have no fingers of their own.

In selecting the appropriate finger on which to wear an astrological ring remember that it should be worn either on its own planetary finger, or it can also be worn upon the finger corresponding to a planet with which it is a permanent friend, particularly if this relationship is strong in the birth-chart. If the relationship between the two planets is both permanent (natural) and temporary (particular to that birth chart), so much the better. For example, someone with an Aries ascendant may want to strengthen their ruling planet due to bad dignity and placement in a weak sign or house, or because of a difficult aspect or conjunction. A Mars gemstone could be worn on either the index finger (Jupiter) or the ring finger (Sun) as both planets are permanent friends of Mars. If in the chart Mars is in the second house from the Sun but in 6th house from Jupiter, Mars would be in temporary friendship with the Sun but in a relationship of a temporary enemy with Jupiter. In this case the ring finger (Sun) should be the one chosen for wearing the Mars gemstone.

An exception to this can arise when there is a choice of using the middle finger (Saturn) or the little finger (Mercury). The middle finger is usually considered preferable to the little finger for wearing a gemstone.

"One should not go out without touching a gem, a respectable person, an auspicious object or a flower." – *The Charaka Samhita 8.19*

Which Hand to Use

There are several considerations to be taken into account when deciding the most appropriate hand to use for wearing an astrological ring.

As there is a natural antagonism between the Sun, Moon, Mars, Jupiter and Ketu on the one hand and Mercury, Venus, Saturn and Rahu on the other, the two groups of stones should not be worn on the same hand. The first group are more suited to being worn on the right hand and the second group on the left hand.

The right hand helps *project* the energies of the planet. It increases the warm, fiery, solar and masculine properties, and relates to the main righthand side energy channel (or *nadi*), known as *Pingala*. This hand is generally more beneficial for masculine planets (Sun, Mars and Jupiter) and planets in masculine /odd signs.

There can be exceptions. For example, if we wanted to increase the energy of Jupiter in Virgo it may be more appropriate to wear the Jupiter gemstone on the left hand, particularly if it were in the first half of that sign (the lunar Hora).

The left hand helps *absorb* the energies of the planet. It increases the lunar and feminine properties, and works on the pathway of the left-side *nadi* of the subtle body known as *Ida*. This hand is usually preferable for feminine planets, Moon and Venus. Any planets in feminine/even signs may be worn on the left hand if preferred.

The planets of neutral gender (Mercury, Saturn, Rahu and Ketu) can be worn on either hand, depending on whether we wish to strengthen their masculine or feminine powers, or whether we wish to enhance their ability to project or absorb. For example, if we have a rather weak Moon that is aspected by a beneficial Jupiter we may wish to enhance the Moons ability to absorb that aspect. In this case the left hand index (Jupiter) finger would be most suitable finger for wearing the Moon's gemstone—a pearl set in a silver ring.

If you are undecided as to which hand to wear the gemstone, don't be unduly concerned. It's considered better to wear the stone on the wrong hand than not to wear it at all.

Wearing a Pendant

A substitute gemstone needs to be larger than the primary gemstone, and is usually more suitable for wearing as a pendant.

Gemstones that are worn in order to improve speech or com- munication, or to ease nervous or respiratory troubles the can be worn around the neck, close to the throat chakra. These will usually be stones ruled by Mercury or by planets placed in the 2nd or 3rd houses (or Taurus and Gemini).

Gemstones that are ruled by planets which increase the heart energy, circulation, emotions or will power (such as the Sun, Moon, Mars or Venus) should be worn close to the heart chakra. As it is impractical to wear the Jupiter or Saturn stones close to their corresponding chakras (the two lowest chakras) it is acceptable to wear them close to the heart chakra. This is because the planets that rule their exaltation signs— Venus rules Libra (Saturn's exaltation) and the Moon rules Cancer (the Moons exaltation sign)—are also related to the heart chakra.

It is also permissible to use a number of small gemstones in the form of a necklace.

Substitute gemstones worn as pendants do not necessarily have to be set in the recommended metals. They can be worn beneath your clothing.

Setting of the Gemstone

Whether worn as a ring or as a pendant all gemstones should be set in such a way that they are in contact with the skin in order for their energies to be effectively transmitted. If worn without touching the skin their effect will be much reduced. This is why ornamental gemstones can be worn that have hardly any detrimental or beneficial effects on the wearer.

In a more general way astrological gemstones can also be kept on a home shrine or altar, in the living room or bedroom, in your car, or wherever you want their protective or enhancing energies to be projected. For this purpose uncut gemstones or crystals may be used.

Purifying and Consecrating Gemstones

All gemstones should be purified and then energized and consecrated to their purpose. There are many ways to cleanse gemstones. The simplest way is to immerse the stone in a liquid overnight. Some good substances for this are:

- For the Sun (Ruby and substitutes), an infusion of calamus.
- For the Moon (Pearl and substitutes), ocean water or milk.
- For Mercury (Emerald and substitutes), an infusion of gotu kola.
- For Mars (Red Coral and substitutes), ocean water or yogurt.
- For Jupiter (Yellow sapphire and substitutes), ghee or calamus infusion.
- For Venus (Diamond and substitutes)—rose water or milk.
- For Saturn (Blue sapphire and substitutes)—infusion of gotu kola or turmeric.
- For Rahu (Hessonite garnet)—turmeric infusion.
- For Ketu (Cat's eye)—calamus infusion.

One way that can be used to purify all gemstones is to soak them overnight in water to which a little sea salt has been added (as a substitute for ocean water), or in an infusion of Gotu Kola (Indian Pennywort), an herb which can be purchased in dried form. Soaking Moon and Venus stones in milk is good.

Once the gem is purified it should be consecrated and empowered by chanting the appropriate planetary mantra while holding the gemstone in your hand. You can also meditate, pray and visualize the results that you wish to bring into your life by wearing the gemstone.

From time to time, under appropriate planetary conditions, gemstones can be cleansed, reconsecrated and/or reenergized.

Planetary Mantras

If there is any doubt regarding the appropriateness or otherwise of wearing a particular gemstone then a safe alternative is to use a planetary mantra. Mantras serve to fortify and balance the energy of a planet in such a way that it brings out its higher, more pure or spiritual qualities. For this reason many yogis and others who are on a spiritual path prefer not to wear gemstones but to use only mantra.

The following are the main mantras for each planet:

For the Sun: *Om sum suryaya namaha*
For the Moon: *Om som somaya namaha* or *Om chum chandraya namaha*
For Mars: *Om kum kujaya namaha*
For Mercury: *Om bum budhaya namaha*
For Jupiter: *Om brahm brihaspataye namaha*
For Venus: *Om shum shukraya namaha*
For Saturn: *Om sham shanaye namaha*
For Rahu: *Om ram rahave namaha*
For Ketu: *Om kem ketave namaha*

Correct pronunciation of the mantras are essential. If in doubt contact your nearest Jyotish Astrologer to be given the correct pronunciation.

Each mantra should be chanted softly or silently 108 times on a daily basis. For this purpose it is best to use an Indian *mala* which consists of 108 beads strung on cord along with a larger bead which acts as a marker bead so that you know when you have completed a full round of 108 repetitions. If you are unable to obtain such beads it is a simple matter to buy 108 wooden beads plus one larger one and to thread them together yourself. Use a strong cord or thread that will not break due to frequent use.

Sitting upright, hold the first bead between the thumb and second finger of the right hand and chant the mantra once. Move the finger and thumb to the second bead and chant the mantra a second time and so on until you reach the 108th bead. Mantra should be chanted with a calm and attentive mind. The focus of the attention should be on the internal sound of the mantra. Early morning is the best time for mantra practice although any regular time when you are unlikely to be interrupted or distracted is suitable.

Each of the mantras given above can be used in one of three ways: (1) In full. (2) Using only the second word of the mantra (the *bija*), or (3) leaving out the second word of the mantra. For example, if using the Sun you could choose the full mantra—*Om Sum Suryaya Namaha,* or just the *bija* mantra—*Sum,* or *Om Suryaya Namaha.*

The first option is best but not for everyone. The second option captures the spirit of the mantra (*bija* means seed, point or essence). Bija Mantras are very potent and very powerful. The third option is the one that is most commonly used.

Timing

Timing is important. The moment that you begin to chant your mantra on a regular basis, or first put on your proper astrological gemstone or pendant to be worn permanently, should be at a time that is in harmony with the cosmic and planetary forces that the stone or mantra represents.

"Ruby is said of the Sun, spotless pearl of the Moon, of Mars coral, of Mercury an emerald, of Jupiter topaz, of Venus diamond, Saturn unblemished sapphire, of the others gomedha and cat's eye." – *Jatika Parijata 2.21*

"The wearing of gemmed ornaments give respect, fame, longevity, wealth, happiness, strength and fruition. Over and above this, it wards off negative astral influences." – *Mani Mala, Part II.122*

Commence wearing a gemstone or using a mantra for the Sun on a Sunday, at sunrise, preferably when the Sun is in a fire sign.

Commence wearing a gemstone or using a mantra for the Moon on a Monday, shortly after sunrise, at a time when the Moon is increasing (waxing) and close to Full Moon. The Moon should be free of malefic aspects and preferably in Taurus, Cancer or Pisces or in the sign of a friendly planet (one ruled by the Sun or Mercury).

Commence wearing a gemstone or using a mantra for Mars on a Tuesday, shortly after sunrise when the Moon is waxing. Mars should be in its own sign or exalted. If this is not possible wait until it occupies the sign of a friendly planet (one ruled by the Sun, Moon or Jupiter).

Commence wearing a gemstone or using a mantra for Mercury on a Wednesday, shortly after sunrise when the Moon is waxing and Mercury is in its own or friendly sign (one ruled by the Sun or Venus). Mercury should not be too close to the Sun (separated by at least 10 degrees).

Commence wearing a gemstone or using a mantra for Jupiter on a Thursday, shortly after sunrise when the Moon is waxing and preferably when Jupiter is in its own, exalted or friendly sign (one ruled by the Sun, Moon or Mars). However, since Jupiter takes a year to transit a sign, this may not always be possible. At the very least Jupiter should be conjunct with or angular to the Moon.

Commence wearing a gemstone or using a mantra for Venus on a Friday, shortly after sunrise when the Moon is waxing and when Venus is in its own, exaltation or friendly signs (those of Mercury or Saturn). Venus should not be closer than 10 degrees to the Sun.

Commence wearing a gemstone or using a mantra for Saturn on a Saturday, shortly after sunrise, during the waxing Moon.

If Saturn is not in a suitable sign (such as one belonging to Mercury or Venus) it should at least be well aspected by Jupiter or by a well placed Venus.

Commence wearing a gemstone or using a mantra for Rahu or Ketu on a Saturday, or on the day of the planet which rules the sign in which it is placed, at a time when the Moon is waxing shortly after sunrise. Ideally Rahu or Ketu should occupy a sign belonging to Mercury or Jupiter or occupy a sign favorable to the planet that rules its natal sign position.

Planetary Hours

Why do we first begin practicing these remedial measures just after sunrise on the appropriate planetary day? Because, beginning from sunrise, each day is divided into 24 planetary hours. The first hour begins at sunrise and is ruled by the same planet that rules the day. Thus Venus rules Friday and it also rules the first planetary hour, which begins at sunrise.

These planetary hours are not necessarily of 60 minutes duration. The time from sunrise to sunset is divided by 12 in order to establish the length of each planetary "hour" during daylight. The same is done with the time that elapses between sunset and sunrise in order to establish the length of the planetary hours during darkness. For example, on a Sunday the first planetary hour commencing at sunrise is ruled by the Sun, the next hour by Venus, followed by the hours of Mercury, Moon, Saturn, Jupiter, Mars, Sun, Venus, Mercury, Moon and Saturn, which concludes at sunset. The sequence continues after sunset with Jupiter, Mars, Sun, Venus, Mercury, Moon, Saturn, Jupiter, Mars, Sun, Venus and Mercury, which brings us to sunrise on Monday. This begins with the Moon, followed by Saturn, and so the sequence continues, with the first planetary hour being ruled by the same planet that rules the planetary day.

Thus on a Sunday there are four planetary hours belonging to the Sun, any of which would be suitable for commencing a solar mantra or for the putting on of a solar gemstone. To avoid the laborious task of making detailed calculations we can be sure that if we have chosen the appropriate day then sunrise or shortly after sunrise will correspond to the appropriate planetary hour.

You now have a good grounding in the basics of the subject, yet, from another perspective, you have only waded a little on the shoreline of the vast ocean that is Jyotish. Regular practice at reading birthcharts will increase your skill and strengthen your deductive and intuitive abilities.

CHAPTER SIXTEEN

PRACTICAL CHART WORK

"The career of a person will be that indicated by the planet ruling the Navamsha sign occupied by the lord of the 10th house from the Lagna, Moon and Sun."

–Brihat Jataka 10:1

In the above quotation the illustrious astrologer Varaha Mihira makes a most interesting observation. It is not necessarily the 10th house of the Rashi chart that will show us a person's natural vocation. The 10th house indicates the degree of recognition and social standing that we may gain in the eyes of others through our career or vocation, but is not always a reliable guide to what that vocation will be. If we take the lord of the 10th house in the Rashi chart and check out the sign that it occupies in the Navamsha chart we will find that the planet ruling that Navamsha sign is a more accurate guide to what that person's true vocation should be.

We are advised to take the 10th from the Lagna, Moon and Sun. This can sometimes give three different planets for judging the career. Matters associated with those three planets can all contribute towards creating an income. In such a case the person is likely to change their occupation several times, or perhaps one of the three planets is much stronger than the other two, in which case that is likely to be the planet that indicates the main occupation.

On the next page is the chart of a rather unorthodox spiritual teacher who is a guru to many. He is a prolific writer and speaks with much authority. His writings are full of insight and inspiration but can be mentally demanding on the reader.

Mercury rules 10th from Lagna and occupies Virgo in the Navamsha.

Thus Mercury is in its own/exaltation sign. This accords with his being the author of many books. His spiritual discourses are precise and detailed and his voice is pleasant to listen to—all Mercury characteristics.

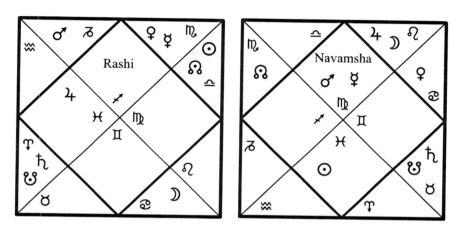

From the Moon Lagna we have Aries ruling the 10th house. Mars joins Mercury in Virgo in the Navamsha—another indication of the influence of Mercury on his vocation.

From the Sun the 10th house is Cancer. In the Navamsha the Moon is in Leo in the 12th with Jupiter. This shows the Sun giving him an unchallenged position of authority in the eyes of his disciples. His appearance and style are authoritative and leonine. He also gives the impression of great authority when he speaks—Mars exalted in Capricorn in the 2nd. There are a variety of interesting yogas to be found in this chart. Hansa Yoga occurs from both the Lagna and the Moon.

In the following chart the person has a career as an artist, so we should expect this to be indicated. The 10th house is ruled by Venus (which aspects the Ascendant from the 7th house). In the Navamsha Venus is in Taurus—its own sign. From the Moon the 10th house is in Pisces, ruled by Jupiter. In the Navamsha chart Jupiter is in Libra, so once again Venus is revealed as being associated with the career. Looking to the

Rashi and Navamsha of an Artist

Sun as Ascendant we find the 10th from the Sun is Capricorn, which is ruled by Saturn. In the Navamsha chart Saturn is weak through being placed in Aries, the sign of its fall. Mars however is in its own sign in the creative 5th house, and in the Rashi chart it is found alongside Venus. All in all a vocation associated with Venus is indicated.

Judgement

Here are some guidelines that will help you develop your astrological skills in chart interpretation. Some of the points have already been made but are repeated herein order to emphasize their importance.

If a house is occupied or aspected by its lord (the planet which rules the sign of the house) it is strengthened, even if the house lord is a malefic.

If a house is occupied by a malefic and is also aspected by another malefic, then the affairs governed by the house are damaged. On the other hand if the tenanting planet is a benefic and is also aspected by another benefic, then the affairs of the house are greatly improved.

A planet that is exalted improves the affairs of the houses that it owns. If a planet is in its own sign then the house that it occupies and the houses that it owns are all benefited.

Whether a benefic or a malefic, the lord of the ascendant surely does not damage any house that it occupies. Thus for a Scorpio ascendant Mars, a natural malefic, also rules the difficult 6th house. Yet if Mars occupies the 5th house it will not damage the affairs of that house.

When examining any house four factors are important: (1) Any planets residing in the house; (2) Any planets aspecting the house under consideration; (3) The placement and condition of the lord of the house; (4) The Karaka for that house. *This last consideration is frequently overlooked, which can often lead to faulty conclusions.*

When judging any house it is also necessary to consider: (1) Whether the lord of the house is well placed in relation to the ascendant; (2) The placement of the lord in relation to the house under consideration; (3) Whether the house being judged is hemmed in by malefic or benefic planets. Let us consider if we are judging the 4th house, even though the 4th lord may be well placed the person could still experience problems and difficulties surrounding such 4th house issues as home, property or happiness if malefics occupy the adjoining houses (for example Saturn in the 3rd and Mars in 5th). Of course if Jupiter occupies the 3rd and Venus is in the 5th then 4th house matters will be greatly benefited. When judging the "hemmed in" position of a house, never go beyond the adjacent signs/houses.

The hemmed in position can also be applied to planets. Thus if instead of the 4th house being hemmed in we may find the 4th lord hemmed in by malefics or benefics. This would have a similar effect to the 4th house being hemmed in, except the effects would be broader— influencing all the areas of life associated with that planet. It is this consideration which gives rise to such yogas as *Ubhachari Yoga* (benefics either side of the Sun) and *Dhurudhara Yoga* (planets either side of the Moon).

Using the Moon Sign as Ascendant

All houses should be considered not only as counted from the Ascendant, but from the Moon sign also. Examining the planetary positions from the Moon, the Ascendant, and from the Sun sign give accurate indications of strong karmic tendencies. Indications that are common to all three perspectives, denote strong karmas. Although not mandatory, Jyotishis consider that if the Moon is stronger than the Ascendant then judgement from the Moon sign should be given preference over the Ascendant. However, since there are no hard and fast rules for determining this distinction and since function of the Ascendant can never be overlooked, it is best to use the Moon sign ascendant *(chandra lagna)* as a secondary point of reference.

We should give particularly close attention to the indications of houses as counted from the Moon sign when (a) the Moon has good paksha bala, (b) it is angular, and/or strongly aspected, (c) it is in its own or exaltation sign, (d) the chart under consideration is that of a female, or (e) if there are many planets in the lunar section of the Hora divisional chart. The greater the number of these factors in any chart the greater will be the significance of using the Moon sign as an alternative Ascendant.

Sage Parashara recommended that the Rising sign, Moon sign and Sun sign should all be considered as separate lagnas in order to correctly judge the houses. Doing this is rather like peeling back the layers of an onion in order to arrive at the center, and while we may have the time to do this with our own birth chart and those of close friends, we don't usually have the time to go through this procedure with every chart that we examine. The same analogy can be applied to the use of division charts— how many readings are given using all sixteen division charts? Not many! Astrological influences are many layered and have many facets.

Illustration of the Importance of
Using the Moon Sign as Ascendant

Here is the chart of Mary Baker Eddy, founder of
"the Christian Science Monitor"

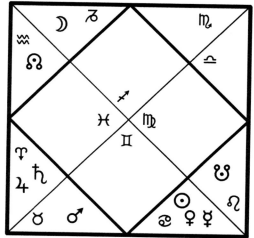

Mary was the author of the renowned "Science and Health", founder of "The Christian Science Monitor" newspaper and of "The Church of Christian Science" (or, more accurately, "The Church of Christ, Scientist") which still has well over 3,000 branches throughout the world.

Data: Mary Baker Eddy; born 16th July 1821; 5:38 p.m.; Bow (near Concord), New Hampshire, USA.

As a child Mary suffered poor health, spending much time confined to her bed. Her ill health continued into her adult life (note the conjunction of her ruling planet Jupiter with Saturn) and it was not until she reached the age of 40 that she experienced any radical improvement in her condition. This recovery was due to her receiving treatment from a well known "mental" healer, Phineas Quimy. Although over the next five years she experienced several relapses. In the winter of 1866 she had a fall in an icy street, which resulted in several severe injuries. Confined to her bed Mary prayed deeply and intensely for a speedy and complete recovery and as a result not only underwent a spontaneous healing but experienced a spiritual awakening that changed the course of her life.

From that time onward she began to develop her spiritual healing practices, discovering that through them she could bring about dramatic healing in others. A charismatic speaker (although not shown in the above chart Uranus and Neptune are in the 1st house), she lectured widely and in 1875 published her famous book "Science and Health" (still in print). In 1879 she founded her Church of Christian Science (still growing) and in 1908 founded the newspaper "Christian Science Monitor" (still being published). Such is a very brief outline of her life.

In Mary's chart, Jupiter, her ruling planet, although placed in the 5th house (enterprise and creative activity), is severely restricted by its close conjunction with Saturn. This accounts for her poor health throughout much of her life, but it also gave her great endurance and self-discipline.

Sagittarius rising and Jupiter in 5th house/Aries gave her a larger than life personality despite the initial limitations caused by the placement of Saturn. Her healing skills are indicated by the fact that Venus, lord of the 6th house (health and healing) is in conjunction with Mercury, lord of the 10th house (profession) in the 8th house (regeneration and transformation).

At first sight there seems little indication of widespread fame and recognition in this chart, *a condition which requires the angular houses to be well emphasized by containing planets.*

In the above chart *all* the angular houses are empty. However, as already mentioned, a basic dictum of Vedic astrology is to consider the Moon sign as a separate Ascendant, particularly if the Moon plays a significant role in understanding the chart.

That 8th house (ruling spiritual regeneration as well as chronic disease and longevity) is heavily tenanted. Being ruled by Cancer it gives added emphasis to the role of the Moon. In fact, as per the rules of Vedic astrology, the Moon also aspects the 8th house and the three planets therein. Notice that the Moon is full, giving it maximum strength. We are therefore justified in using the sign containing the Moon as a secondary Ascendant.

This helps us gain greater confluence of influences. When we view the chart in this light, using the Moon sign (Capricorn) as the Ascendant, we find that more than half the planets will occupy angular (kendra) houses and that the lord of the 10th house (governing fame and recognition) from the Moon, as well as the lords of the lunar 8th and 9th houses occupy the 7th and fully aspect the lunar Ascendant.

As someone who lectured widely, wrote a very influential book and founded a newspaper (all 3rd house activities) we would expect to find a strong link between the 1st and 3rd houses. Whether we use the Rising sign or the Moon sign as the Ascendant, in both cases we find the 1st and 3rd lords in conjunction. Rahu (North Node) in the 3rd house/Aquarius indicates that she needed to fulfill her desires through radical reforming (Aquarian) activities of the type that we associate with these houses. Ketu (South Node) in 9th house/Leo indicates that she worked at developing spiritual principles and practices in a previous incarnation and that her organizational skills and qualities of leadership (Leo) where also inherited from the past.

Angular Planets

Planets in angular or kendra houses gain in strength. Natural benefics so placed are capable of giving strong positive results and malefics of being problematic. Of all the angular houses the most powerful is the 10th.

Any planets within 10° either side of the Ascendant axis or the M.C. axis are particularly potent.

If cardinal signs (Aries, Cancer, Libra and Capricorn) are on the cusps of the angular houses they make one more active, persistent and dynamic in nature. If fixed signs (Taurus, Leo, Scorpio and Aquarius) are on the cusps of the angular houses the person becomes more fixed in their attitudes and outlook on life. They are more sedentary and less inclined to travel or movement. If mutable signs (Gemini, Virgo, Sagittarius and Pisces) fall on the angular cusps the person becomes more mentally active.

They are cooperative and adaptable but are also capable of manifesting qualities common to either of the other two groups. This is because the first 15° of mutable signs have qualities similar to the fixed signs while the last 15° have more in common with the cardinal signs.

Neecha bhanga: Cancellation of Debility

A planet in the sign of its fall is said to be *neecha* or debilitated. Planets that are in the sign of their fall have the influence of this adverse condition cancelled out if:

- an exalted planet occupies the same sign as the fallen planet.
- the lord of the sign occupied by the fallen planet is exalted.
- the lord of the sign occupied by the fallen planet is in an angle (kendra) from the Moon or Ascendant.
- the ruler of the house which is occupied by the fallen planet aspects that planet.
- the planet which would be exalted if it was in the sign occupied by the fallen planet is in an angle to the Moon or Ascendant.

These points are important and should be memorized. This can also work the other way around. For instance, an exalted planet can be damaged if the lord of the sign that the exalted planet occupies is in its fall.

On the next page is an example of how *Neecha bhanga* operate in Albert Einstein's horoscope. We observe that mutable signs fall on the kendra (angular) houses. This made him mentally agile. The lord of the 5th house (intelligence) is exalted in the 10th. Mercury, lord of the 4th house (formal education) is in the sign of its fall and placed between two malefics—he left school at 15 with very poor grades and failed to gain any distinction as a result of attending university. Yet because Mercury is in the sign of an exalted planet, its debilitated condition is cancelled, so that eventually the manifestation of his Mercury qualities became his strength.

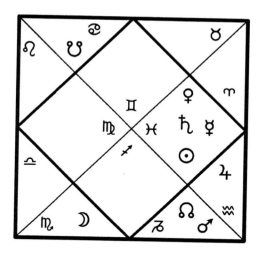

The cancellation of Mercury's debilitation is also reinforced by Jupiter, the lord of the sign occupied by Mercury, being angular to the Moon (see previous page for *Neecha bhanga* rules).

The Moon is another planet that although in the sign of its fall becomes strengthened by its ruler (Mars) being placed in its sign of exaltation (Capricorn). If we take the Moon sign as an ascendant we find that 5th house (intelligence) is occupied by an exalted Venus in Pisces. Still using the Moon ascendant we also observe that the 5th house lord, Jupiter, is aspecting the 10th house.

Taking the Sun sign as a separate ascendant we find that the Moon governs the solar 5th house, and that this is placed in the 9th house from the Sun. Because the Moon has *neecha bhanga* (cancellation of debility due to being in its fall) we can conclude that Einstein's chart shows great intelligence according to all three Ascendants.

CHAPTER SEVENTEEN

THE YOGA SUTRAS OF PATANJALI

All astrology deals with the likely outcomes of past actions: the way our actions contribute to the experience of our outer environment, condition our body, emotions and thoughts, and thus determine our character and personality traits. If this was all that had to be considered astrology would be an exact science. Our past activities would completely condition our future. But we are more than the body, emotions and mental traits with which we so often identify ourselves.

We are all blessed by freewill and our lives are largely shaped by the interplay of fate (karma) and freewill. We all have freedom of choice and the extent and manner to which we exercise this ability determines the extent to which our lives are conditioned by astrological influences. No one should feel completely conditioned by their past karma (which is indicated by the positions of the planets in our horoscope).

Certainly past karmic influences will arise and our lives are shaped by the choices we have to make. However, our future is determined and unfolds from our consciousness and mental states. These continually modify the future that is suggested by the birth chart, which has much to say about our subconscious conditioning but less to say about the consequences of our taking control of our lives and becoming more Self-determined.

The Yoga Sutras of Patanjali, although primarily a treatise on the practice of Samadhi, contains a wealth of knowledge for the Vedic astrologer. An astrologer who practices and properly comprehends the message within the Yoga Sutras is better equipped to counsel those who are seeking guidance. Study and meditation on the Yoga Sutras serves to develop and provide concise knowledge on the most efficient means of transcending the karmic condition.

While a study of the complete Yoga Sutras of Patanjali is advised, the following select verses and commentary will help clarify the above train of thought:

I.2-3 Yoga is the process of ending fluctuations and changes in the field of consciousness. Then the seer abides in its own nature.

In this context, the term yoga refers to samadhi. Samadhi is the bringing together of awareness, the stilling of the restless identification with external phenomena. When changes in the field of consciousness cease, the Seer, or the individualized unit of pure consciousness exists as it is.

This is the ultimate aim of yoga practice and also the intention behind Vedic astrology. When, through astrological counsel, people are properly guided in fulfilling their station in life, living in harmony with the forces of nature, and practicing soul liberating techniques to fully realize the wholeness of life, their field of consciousness becomes calm. The eternal Self then shines through.

I.4-5 Otherwise there is conformity to definitions. They are obstructing, pain causing, or non-obstructing, not pain causing.

In the current age, the normal human experiences fragmented awareness. Awareness that is fragmented misidentifies with everything that passes before it. Every thought, emotion, circumstance, relationship, and subconscious tendency are taken to be the person's real Self. When these transient phenomena pass, suffering or happiness may result, depending on the nature of the object being perceived.

The planetary energies provide the force that triggers and sustains our varied experiences in life. They continue to cast forth supporting energy to maintain these experiences as long as there is a form to hold the energy. Our attachment and identification provides that form, and so a person's fragmented awareness, alternating between pleasure and pain, persists.

I.12 The ending of those definitions occurs by practice of yoga and non-attachment.

Consistent yoga practice results in freedom from conformity to the soul binding definitions of fragmented awareness. Nonattachment to what occurs within the field of our consciousness allows the planets to exhaust their hold on our awareness. This equates to freedom from karmic planetary forces.

 Note that nonattachment is not simply aloofness or trying to ignore the obvious. We are attached when we compulsively desire something to be present within our awareness. We are also attached when we strongly want to get something out of our field of awareness. When we can remain as the observer, the Seer, not identified with anything within our field of awareness we are free. The planets exhaust their force, and once that is complete we can then direct our lives more easily in a worthwhile way.

I.23-24 Samadhi is also near when there is perfect alignment with Ishvara. Ishvara, which is untouched by karma, is distinguishable from the root obstructions of consciousness that cause pain.

Ishvara can be translated from Sanskrit as the ultimate Seer, Presence, or God. Creation flows from Ishvara. By aligning attention with Ishvara in Yogic meditation and at other times when engaged in activities a person then identifies with the creator rather than the creation. The creator is not touched by its creation. And so it follows that when we identify with our karma and the planetary forces within creation, we experience those things. When we identify with the creator, we do not.

 Although astrology can be used to predict and ascertain the nature of mundane circumstances, we need to remember that it is ultimately a spiritual science. When an astrologer identifies with Ishvara the astrologer can then see with the eye of God, or see from a divine perspective, which is vaster than the limited viewpoint of the ego personality.

 From that vantage point, counsel of greatest benefit can be given to the person seeking guidance, and for the whole of creation.

This sutra also reflects one of the prime remedial measures under utilized in the prescription of alleviating planetary karma.

I.27-29 The inner sound current (OM) is the expression of Ishvara. Repetition of the inner sound current (OM) leads to realization of its meaning. From that comes the realization of an inwardly directed consciousness, and the elimination of obstacles.

One way to perfectly align attention with Ishvara is by use of the light and sound current meditation described in the chapter on meditation.

II.12-13 Unconscious and subconscious impressions may result in the manifestation of unplanned experiences in this and other life cycles. As long as the causes of effects (karma) reside in the unconscious, their influence can manifest according to species and span of life, and in relationship to perceptions of pleasure or pain.

For the most part, neither astrology nor intuition is needed to ascertain the general direction of a person's life. We go through the same actions and experience the same situations over and over again. Even our mental and emotional states are fairly predictable. To determine the general future, we can look at the general qualities of the past. If no changes are made to alter the course then life will continue as it has.

Sometimes events occur that are beyond our understanding, beyond our ability to compartmentalize into our general concept of life. These are caused by subconscious impressions within our mind and consciousness. They are like seeds planted below surface of our shallow awareness. If the seeds are not dug up by yoga and meditation practice, they will sprout and grow when they are provided suitable circumstances for germination.

Without astrology, these can be discovered and uprooted directly through Self-inquiry. For those currently unable to practice intensive transformational methods of Self-inquiry, an astrologer can reveal these subconscious tendencies and the time line on which they will likely manifest. The astrologer can then recommend specific remedies to neutralize unpleasant effects.

II.16 Pain and suffering which are not yet manifested is to be avoided.

Through consultation with enlightened men and women, by our own yoga practice, and through the exploration of astrological influences we can avoid pain. All three are known means to end suffering. That is how it is avoided.

II.17 Suffering is due to the souls mistaken sense of Self.

Enlightened teachers direct us to our real eternal Self. Meditation practice calms our mind and awareness directly revealing our Self. A gifted astrologer describes the planetary influences at hand and ahead, and encourages us to align our attention with Ishvara and to merge in our real Self, where karmas do not exist. A gifted astrologer shares enlightenment by showing the methods and appropriate modes of living that will reveal our real Self, based on our individual karmic situation.

II.24 Imperfect awareness of its own nature is the cause of the soul's identification with matter.

Just as a family or a society may hold beliefs about the nature of life that are false and defend them as if they are the gospel truth, so too do individuals have faulty beliefs. *The worst of those beliefs is that we are a transient human personality held in the thrall of forces that we cannot control.* By never questioning or exploring the validity of this notion we remain trapped in self fulfilling prophecy. Our awareness is imperfect regarding who we really are, and so we identify with material things.

It is only out of habit that we identify with our planets and the results they create within our life situation. We have all agreed to participate in the drama of life.

We are only actors and yet we identify so intensely with the part we are playing, that we forget our true Self. Through yoga meditation, Self-inquiry, and living in accord with natural law do we wake up from the dream, or at least realize we are the dreamer.

II.28 By practicing the eight limbs of yoga, as the impurities diminish, there is a light of knowing leading to discrimination.

Identifying with what we are not indicates ignorance. By purifying our awareness we begin to see things more clearly. The truth concerning life and its orderly processes is revealed. This occurs through yoga practice.

Complete practice of yoga, of which there are eight aspects, removes the impurities that block realization of spiritual freedom. First, the impurities are removed. As these impurities dissolve our powers of discrimination develop. Discrimination is essential to fully comprehend the knowledge that unfolds from within us to impart our total spiritual freedom.

Knowledge of the eternal Self is compared to light in this sutra. As the particles of ignorance are wiped away from the spotlight of divine grace through dedicated yoga practice, the light of knowing shines forth freely. Once the particles of ignorance are gone, then the planets are unable to grasp us, because there is nothing left to grasp. We are then free.

II.29 Yama, niyama, asana, pranayama, pratyahara, dharana, dhyana, and samadhi are the eight limbs.

The eight aspects to be practiced are: refraining from harmful behaviors, cultivating life-enhancing behaviors, developing steady meditation posture, practice of scientific breathing techniques, inward flowing of attention from the senses, focused attention, meditation, and cognitive absorption. Synergistic application of all eight limbs removes the ignorance that binds us to the planets.

The harmful behaviors to refrain from include: violence, falsehood, stealing, wasting vital resources, and possessiveness. If these tendencies are within us, it only takes common sense to realize that they will cause trouble. If they are within us and we are unconscious of their power then when the planets strike our psyche in certain ways, we will experience their expression and the results that come from that expression.

By cultivating the opposite qualities (peace, truth, prosperity consciousness, conserving our resources, and non-attachment), through dedicated intention the forces of negativity are lessened and finally dissolved. Again, leaving nothing harmful for the planets to stimulate.

By practicing the niyamas, which include purity, contentment, intensity in spiritual practice, mantra, and alignment of attention with the Ishvara , the higher qualities of the planetary forces are allowed to express. These are the sattvic cosmic forces that permeate the universe. Sattva is one of the three primary forces of nature representative of light, clarity, orderliness and peace.

The practice of asana gives control over the restlessness of the body and it supports our health and immune system. Here we can imagine how karmas do not need to be triggered and that no drastic remedial measures are needed because a simple change of lifestyle would do the trick. If a person has a weak immune system due to inactivity or improper eating, and they are doing nothing, chances are likely that any genetic predisposition to disease will manifest. The planets can trigger any disease indicated by the chart. However, by practicing hatha yoga asanas the person will stimulate vital forces and strengthen the body. The chances of illness to manifest, although the potential did exist are greatly lessened.

This needs to be remembered, because if an unhealthy person desires an astrological remedial measure to improve the health and they are not making any choices in life to support health, the first remedial measure should be to encourage them to adopt a healthy lifestyle. Practical, basic how to live, advice is always the best first step. Then if they are still having trouble, a mantra, gem or rudraksha mala can be advised and additionally supportive. This applies to both mental and physical health.

Pranayama includes breathing exercises that actively aim to pacify the mind and cleanse the energetic channels within the body. Sushumna breathing, as described earlier in this text is one such pranayama method that can be used. Another helpful pranayama practice is alternate nostril breathing, which can be learned from a trained yoga teacher.

Pratyahara, dharana, dhyana and samadhi are all higher internal practices. Once a person has gained proficiency in the previous limbs then more focus can be given to these aspects of yoga. Mastery of the first four limbs will make practice of the last four much easier.

Pratyahara is turning attention away from sense involvement and directing it within. Dharana is concentration. Dhyana is meditation. Samadhi is direct experience within unified awareness. By turning attention within we are releasing our involvement with the transient world of creation and its influences, which includes removing identification from planetary forces. Dharana allows our minds to become steady and one pointed. Then we can maintain the practice of meditation. Once meditation becomes stable and concentration is consistent, then only our chosen object of meditation fills our awareness. All else drops away, and our unified awareness dawns.

It is recommended to meditate on that which is beyond creation and the planetary influences. These include Ishvara, OM, or Pure Consciousness. Whatever your awareness unites with, that is what you will experience.

III.23 By contemplation on karmic influences which are slow or fast in producing effects, knowledge of the causes of one's death, or that of others, and other unusual occurrences can be acquired.

Contemplating the influences within the chart allows the astrologer to gain insight into the karmic states and the timing of their expression. Some planets move quickly by transit such as Mercury, Mars, Venus, and the Moon. Others are slower in their scouring of the natal chart. These include Jupiter, Saturn, Rahu, and Ketu.

By contemplating the relationship between the birth chart and the current planetary positions, as well as the time of the planetary cycles, called the Dasha sequence, the astrologer can see the unusual occurrences in one's life.

III.26 By projecting attention and awareness into the cosmic field of Supreme Consciousness, that which is veiled, subtle or remote can be known.

An astrologer who practices yoga meditation and contemplates Ishvara, OM, or Pure Consciousness can abide within that cosmic field. From this vantage point, their awareness can be directed to veiled, subtle, or remote areas. These include the future, the past, and one's internal karmic condition.

The verses of the Yoga Sutras in Chapter 3, deal with soul powers. It is important to note that these develop as one purifies their consciousness and gains greater identification with their true Self. The powers can be generated through effort and will, but that does not result in clarity of awareness. First one clarifies their awareness and then, if the powers are needed in this life, they will manifest.

As an astrologer, the quality that needs developed first and foremost is clarity of consciousness and surrender of the illusional sense of Self. When this occurs, the ego is not seeking astrological knowledge for its own gain. The soul is manifesting in creation in a form of service, that of practicing astrology. With this purity of motive, the necessary soul powers blossom.

III.27-29 Contemplation on the sun provides knowledge of celestial bodies and categories and processes of cosmic manifestation. Contemplation on the moon and planets provides knowledge of their relationship and movement. Contemplation on the Pole Star provides knowledge of the relationships and movements of the stars.

Whatever we contemplate with alert expectation of discovery, we can realize within our consciousness. By meditating on the orb of the sun, the moon, the planets and the pole star, this will provide accurate and direct insight of astrological knowledge. A Self-realized and skilled astrologer does not need the chart to practice astrology. He or she can turn within and by contemplating on what needs to be known, taps into the internal solar system and gains the information needed.

To meditate on these astrological bodies can be done in many ways. One can meditate in the sun, and contemplate its light, heat, and radiance. One can gaze at the moon and let all thoughts drop away as the visual sight of the moon in the sky becomes the object of meditation. Spending time at night outside meditating on the vastness of space and contemplating the night sky with its countless stars is also effective.

Remember the inner solar system as well. One does not need to go outside and actually see the material phenomena. Remember what the sun looks like and hold a vision of it in your spiritual eye. Do the same with the moon, planets and stars. By doing this, insights arise as to the nature and state of the cosmos, both internal and external.

Also note, the Pole Star is a term used by various yoga teachers to represent the spinal pathway.

IV.8 The forces and tendencies of mental impressions are manifested when pervading circumstances are most suitable for their unfoldment.

Tendencies and mental impressions are like seeds. Seeds do not sprout immediately. When the circumstances are correct they begin to grow. If the circumstances are maintained, they eventually grow into a robust weed or flower. The same holds true for our astrological influences. The chart may indicate good fortune or troubles in general regarding certain areas of life, but these will only occur when the right circumstances are present. That is why the transits of planets through the sky and the planetary cycles are so important. They indicate when those circumstances will be available to trigger the stored responses within us.

This is also helpful for the astrologer because counsel can be given to avoid certain activities during difficult times.

Although the transits and planetary cycles may indicate a malicious event, avoiding situations that would provide the right circumstances for the event's occurrence can prevent this. For example, if a pattern for heart disease or cancer is seen within the chart, a healthy diet and lifestyle will do much to change the possibility of health issues.

The same can be said for positive influences. Good times to heal, to get married, to move, or to start a business can all be indicated within the chart. Making intentional actions during those time periods help make the undertaking more auspicious.

IV.11 Karmic influences exist because of a mistaken sense of Self and the support of objects of perception. In their absence, karmic influences disappear.

This is a key to the healing aspect of astrology. By turning attention to our Self and resting our attention there, we cannot simultaneously be aware of outer conditioning factors. The planets are such a factor. The more stable a person is established in identifying with the essence of being, the less planetary forces will be of influence. Maintaining awareness on the Self, the karmic planetary influences, having nothing to cling to, eventually disappear.

One of the reasons people repeat certain experiences throughout life are due to their identification with those influences. It serves to strengthen the false sense of self.

IV.12 Subliminal impressions and memories of past perceptions of events exist with the potential for future events to occur. How future events unfold is determined by one's path in life.

Our birth chart represents nothing but the environment that we have created by the karmic pattern that was determined by our pastlife actions. According to this karmic pattern we are attracted to be reborn at a given time that is favorable to that pattern.

What is to be, is not necessarily what has to be. Karma can govern the destiny indicated in the birth chart, but karma is governed by the exercise of our free will and divine determination, which can change the course of events in our life, or at least mitigate adverse aspects.

Contemplation of these sutras and their meaning after meditation practice, will allow the reader to fully grasp the aspect of reality that is Vedic Astrology.

GLOSSARY

Amrita – One of the treasures emanated from the galactic churning. The nectar of immortality.

Artha – One of the four goals of human life, to be able to procure necessary wealth and resources.

Ascendant – The first house of the birth chart. The sign rising on the Eastern horizon at birth.

Aspect – The influence of a planet directed at another area of the chart.

Atma – Self. The absolute reality of the universe.

Ayanamsha – The longitudinal difference between the tropical and sidereal zodiac.

Ayurveda – The natural medicine system of India based on the three doshic, or constitutional types called Pitta, Vata, and Kapha. "Ayur" means life and "veda" means knowledge.

Bhava – The Sanskrit term for "house" in Vedic Astrology.

Bhukti – The 2nd level of the Dasha sequence, after the Mahadasha.

Cardinal – The outgoing and enterprising signs: Aries, Cancer, Libra, and Capricorn.

Chakra – Centers of life force energy along the spinal pathway. This is also a term used in India for the Birth Chart.

Chara – Cardinal.

Combustion – The condition of a planet too close to the sun, often weakening the significations represented by the planet.

Conjunction – Commingling of planetary energies when two or more planets occupy the same house.

Cusp – The middle of a house.

Dasha – A planetary cycle in which a particular planet will give its results through time. The results depend on the situation of the planets within the birth chart.

Dasamsa – The 10th divisional chart, the *Dasamsa*, provides additional information regarding a person's career.

Debilitation – A planet is in the sign of its fall. Here it is weak and has little power to do good.

Dharma – One's duty and purpose in the world.

Divisional Chart – These are similar to the Harmonic charts developed by the astrologer John Addey, which were partially inspired by his studies of the divisional charts of Vedic astrology. Vedic astrologers can use up to 15 divisional charts, all of which are derived from the main *(rashi)* chart, each one giving a deeper insight into a particular area of a person's life.

Dosha – There are three basic constitutions, or *doshas*, which arise out of the five elements (earth, water, fire, air and ether). Earth and water give rise to Kapha, Fire gives rise to Pitta and when air combines with ether it gives rise to Vata.

Drekkana – The *Drekkana* chart has affinities the third house in that it relates to brothers and sisters. It also indicates our courage, energy, motivation and the ability to achieve our goals and ambitions, particularly those that require enterprise and initiative.

Drishti – *Drishti* is the ability of a planet to project its energy to other areas of the chart by influencing signs of the zodiac other than the one in which it resides.

Dusthana – The 6th 8th and 12th houses are considered inauspicious. They carry negative energies related to, among other things, disease (6th), death (8th) and loss (12th). In Sanskrit these three houses are referred to as *Dusthana* or *Trik* indicating that they are houses associated with sorrow or suffering.

Dwadamsha – the 12th division chart provides insight into one's parents, ancestral heritage and past life karma.

Dwara – Mutable or dual signs.

Ephemeris – A table or book that gives the values of astrological objects and their placements in the sky.

Exultation – The highest manifestation of a planetary energy occurs when in the sign of its exultation. Here the planet is strong and powerful.

Fall – See debilitation.

Fixed – Signs that are intense, steadfast and resistant to sudden change, Taurus, Leo, Scorpio and Aquarius.

Graha – Sanskrit term for planet. Means, "that which grasps or seizes".

Gyana – Wisdom.

Hora – Second divisional chart. The *Hora* chart has a connection to the 2nd house of the Rashi chart, and for this reason is said to be related to wealth.

House – One-twelfth division of the zodiac. The sign rising on the Eastern Horizon at the time of birth indicates the 1st house. The next sign indicates the 2nd house, and so on.

Jaimini – Sage and highly respected authority in Vedic Astrology.

Jyotish – India's name for her science of Astrology. Loosely translated to "science of light."

Jyotishi – One who practices Jyotish.

Kama – One of the four goals of human life. Enjoyment.

Kapha – Ayurvedic Dosha created from the Earth and Water element.

Karaka – Planetary significator for specific areas of life.

Karma – An influence that causes or may cause an effect. Accumulated habits, tendencies and conditioning from repeated ways of thinking and acting.

Kendra – Houses 1, 4, 7, and 10. The angular houses of the chart. After the 1st house/Ascendant, the most vital and important houses are the 4th, 7th and 10th. Any planets in the 7th and 10th houses will have a direct impact on the Ascendant, although planets in any of these four angular houses will have a considerable influence on one's life. Planets placed in the 10th house are often the most influential planets in the whole chart and their importance should never be underestimated.

Ketu – The south node of the moon. The body created when Rahu was decapitated. Karaka of liberation.

Kona – Angular house.

Krishna paksha – The dark half of the month. Term used to indicate a waning moon.

Kundali – The term used in India for Birth Chart.

Lahiri Ayanamsha – The most commonly used Ayanamsha. The Lahiri *Ayanamsha* is also known as the *Chaitrapaksha Ayanamsha*.

Mantra – A sequence of sounds that have a vibrational influence that modifies the manner in which a planets energy becomes manifest.

Maraka – It literally means "killer" although its real meaning in an astrological context is the propensity to cause death or to be detrimental to our health or longevity.

The *maraka* houses are the 2nd and the 7th. This is because the 7th house is 12th from the 8th (longevity).

Moksha – The fourth goal of human life, meaning liberation of consciousness.

Moolatrikona – A planet in *moolatrikona* (*moola*, root; *trikona*, triangle) is considered stronger than when its own sign but not quite so elevated or as powerful as when in its exultation.

Mutable – Mutable *(dwiswabhava)* signs are variable and adaptable.

Nakshatra – In Vedic astrology the Zodiac also divided into 27 stellar constellations known as the Lunar Mansions, Astrims or *Nakshatras*. These too have their initial starting point at 0° Aries, which marks the beginning of *Ashwini*, the first of the *Nakshatras*.

Navamsha – Corresponds with the 9th Harmonic chart now used by some Western astrologers. The *Navamsha* is nearly as important as the *Rashi* or main sign chart, and gives additional information regarding long term relationships. It is also used to determine whether the indications of the natal chart is going to manifest with difficulty or ease. Esoteric astrologers regard the *Navamsha* as the horoscope of the soul, and the *Rashi* or main sign chart as representing the outer and more mundane conditions of a person's life.

Neecha – Another term used to indicate debilitation or fall.

Nodes – Rahu and Ketu are the north and south nodes of the moon. They indicate the point in the sky where the moon's orbit around the earth intersects the ecliptic. These are the points where eclipses occur.

Paksha Bala – The changing cycle of the moon's strength. *Paksha-bala* gradually increases and decreases over the course of the lunar month, yet for practical purposes the Moon is considered weak by some astrologers if its distance from the Sun is less than 90 degrees. If the moon's distance is greater than 120 degrees from the Sun it is considered very good.

Pitta – The Ayurvedic dosha ruled by the fire element.

Prishtodaya – A sign that rises with its back. The back-rising or *prishtodaya* signs are Aries, Taurus, Cancer, Sagittarius and Capricorn.

Prakruti – One's natural constitution *(prakruti),* indicating the aggravating dosha(s) and particular constitutional weaknesses.

Rahu – The North Node of the moon.

Raja Yoga Karaka – A planet owning both an angular house (1st, 4th, 7th or 10th) and a trinal house (5th or 9th) attaining a very important and positive status.

Rashi – The main birth chart from which all other harmonic charts are derived. The Natal Chart.

Retrograde – A retrograde planet refers to a visual phenomenon that occurs due to different speeds of the planets in relation to the earth. When this happens to a planet its speed decreases until it appears to become stationary. It will then appear to be moving backwards (retrograde) through the zodiac for a period of time.

Rising Sign – See Ascendant.

Sandhi – Any planet found in the very beginning or end of a sign ($0°$ or $29°$) is considered to be weakened due to being placed at the junction point of two signs. If the junction point occurs between a water and a fire sign this is considered to be particularly inauspicious, this area being referred to as *gandanta*.

Sanskrit – The religious and classical ancient language of India.

Sanyasi – One who lives in the world without any material attachments or possessions.

Shadvarga – The most used of the division charts are the *Hora, Drekkana, Navamsha Dwadamsha* and *Trimsamsa*. Of these five the most important is undoubtedly the *Navamsha* chart, which, in a Vedic horoscope, is nearly always shown alongside the main Rashi chart. Including the *Rashi* chart these are referred to as the *Shadvargas* or six divisional charts.

Shirshodaya – A sign that rises with its front. The front-rising or *shirshodaya* signs are Gemini, Virgo, Leo, Libra, Scorpio and Aquarius.

Shukla paksha – The bright half of the month when the moon is waxing.

Sidereal Zodiac – Vedic astrology uses the Sidereal or "fixed" zodiac, which is the one that corresponds to the actual star constellations.

Sign – A constellation of the Zodiac.

Sthira – Fixed *(sthira)* signs are intense, steadfast and resistant to sudden change.

Tajika – *Tajika* aspects were expounded in detail by Neelakantha, an Indian astrologer who lived during the 16th century. These are the very same aspects as the five major aspects (conjunction, opposition, square, trine and sextile) used in Western astrology, which measures aspects from planet to planet rather than from planet to sign. The orbs (the allowance of deviation from an exact aspect) used by Neelakantha are exactly the same as those recommended by William Lilly, the 17th century English astrologer.

Trik – The 6th 8th and 12th houses are considered inauspicious. They carry negative energies related to, among other things, disease (6th), death (8th) and loss (12th). In Sanskrit these three houses are referred to as *Dusthana* or *Trik* indicating that they are houses associated with sorrow or suffering.

Trimamsa – The *Trimsamsa* (or 30th Harmonic) is rather different from the other divisional charts. For a start it seems to have little to do with the division of a sign by 30. It consists of 5 unequal division and lacks any reference to Cancer or Leo. Never-the-less this is an important division chart for understanding major health issues or periods of misfortune.

Tropical Zodiac – The "moving" zodiac used mainly in Western Astrology, that does not take into consideration the natural precession of the constellations.

Ubhayodaya – Pisces is said to have the characteristics of both front and back rising signs and is known as "both-ways rising" or *ubhayodaya.*

Upachaya – The 3rd, 6th, 10th and 11th houses are also referred to as *upachaya,* a Sanskrit term which means "increasing" or "improving," as any planets placed in these house tends to increase in strength and influence with the passage of time. This especially applies to the 11th house, where planets gradually strengthen and improve in quality and influence.

Uucha – See Exultation.

Vata – The Ayurvedic dosha ruled by the combined air and ether elements.

Vedic – Meaning of the Vedas. Self-revealed knowledge.

Vimshotari Dasha – The most widely used method is the *Vimshotari Dasha* system, also known as *Udu Dasha*. Sage Parashara, the great authority on Vedic astrology describes a variety of dasha systems (over 30) in his classic "Brihat-Para-shara-Hora-Shastra", yet gives the greatest attention to expounding the *Vimshotari* system.

Yoga – In Jyotish, a yoga means a combination. Usually this is a particular combination of two or more planets, although it can also mean a combination of a planet and sign or a planet and house, often involving the aspect of another planet. Sometimes more than two planets are involved, so that if one where to list all the various yogas given in the classical texts the number would run into thousands.

ABOUT THE AUTHORS

Richard Fish

In the early 1970s Richard made an intensive study of astrology. Having also studied under various Vedic teachers and astrologers, in 1977 he was awarded the degree and title of Jyotishnatak by Sri Visvanartha Deva Sarma, founder of the Viswa Jyotirvid Samgha. He has taught and practiced both Western and Vedic systems of astrology, as well as Hastha vidya (astropalmistry) and Prasna (horary astrology).

As a Kriya-yogi and an ordained minister of The Center for Spiritual Awareness, Richard also teaches Kriya Yoga meditation techniques, considering the practice of yoga to be the true "inner astrology."

Richard lives in the village of Burtle, eight miles west of Glastonbury in Somerset. See: www.kriyayogacentre.org.uk.

Ryan Kurczak

Ryan Kurczak graduated from Fairmont State University with a bachelor's degree in Psychology and minor in Philosophy. After college he attended the Mountain State School of Massage, and completed training with The American Institute of Vedic Studies and the European Institute of Vedic Studies in the subjects of Yoga, Ayurveda and Jyotish. He has studied astrology intensively under Richard Fish and Ernst Wilhelm.

Ryan was initiated by Roy Eugene Davis, a direct disciple of Paramahansa Yogananda. He teaches group meditation and Kriya Yoga practices, at various Yoga and New Thought Centers, and works with sincere students individually.

He lives in Asheville, NC where he works full-time as a Vedic Astrologer, offering phone and internet astrological sessions.

See: www.AshevilleVedicAstrology.com.

Other Books By The Authors

By Richard Fish and Ryan Kurczak

The Art and Science of Vedic Astrology Vol. II:
Intermediate Techniques and Applied Chart
Assessment
(September 2013)

By Ryan Kurczak

Kriya Yoga:
Continuing the Lineage of Enlightenment
(September 2012)

A Course In Tranquility:
Integrating Spiritual Practice, Effective Living,
& Non Duality
(October 2012)

CPSIA information can be obtained at www.ICGtesting.com
Printed in the USA
LVOW08s0219130116

470297LV00001B/128/P